SUPERVISING THE ELECTRONIC OFFICE

SUPERVISING THE ELECTRONIC OFFICE

Caroline Blaazer and Eric Molyneux

Gower
with
Philips Business Systems

Published by
Gower Publishing Company Limited
Aldershot, Hants, England.

British Library Cataloguing in Publication Data

Blaazer, Caroline
    Supervising the electronic office.
    1. Office Practice – Automation
    2. Office management
    I. Title II.   Molyneux, Eric
    651   HF5548.2

    ISBN 0-566-02448-9

Phototypesetting by Graphic Studios (Southern) Limited, 16B High Street, Godalming, Surrey.

Printed in Great Britain at the University Press, Cambridge

Contents

Foreword

by *John Garnett,* CBE, Director, The Industrial Society

The Industrial Society has always taken an active part in obtaining people's co-operation with innovation at work. The changes brought about by the increasing use of electronics in the office have faced us with yet another challenge to grasp. This is the challenge of using microtechnology for the good of all. It is the challenge of ensuring that the technology does what we want it to do.

People's jobs are bound to change. Some jobs may disappear, and others will take their places. Yet the great universal truths remain, one of which is that the supervisor's job is as important as it ever was, taking the lead as the first level of management.

The supervisor should still be the person who is in charge at the bottom, with the responsibility of getting the best out of people, of getting them to co-operate with change, and of using practical, action-based leadership skills to increase motivation and commitment to the job.

Electronics in the office are designed to speed workflow and to become the new tools of the trade. This book provides a clear, practical guide to supervisors who need to get the best out of people, and to help people live with and make the best of the new equipment which they use.

Preface

There are countless excellent books on general
supervisory skills, and there are plenty of books and
articles which explain the way a computer works.
The present volume aims to fill the gap between
these two elements by providing a practical guide for
supervisors who work in an electronic office.

Many supervisors flounder helplessly among rows
of VDUs with bored staff and makeshift office
furniture. Usually they lack guidance and support
from their superiors in the man-management skills
they need to get the best from people who work in an
electronic office. These offices often appear
unfriendly, cold and almost impossible to
understand. Far too many supervisors seem resigned
to being servants of both the DP department and the
VDU screen.

This book is a direct outcome of the courses run
regularly by The Industrial Society on the skills
needed in 'supervising the electronic office'. These
courses are sponsored by Philips Business Systems,
with whose help they were originally developed.
The book covers the subjects at the heart of the
courses, including an understanding of the
technology and the DP department, the role of the
supervisor vis-à-vis the specialists and the rest of the

organisation, the management of change, motivation, communication, training, and health and safety in the office.

We have tried to provide, in written form, as much as possible of the information given on the courses. What we cannot provide is the priceless collected experience which comes out of group exercises which form a vital part of the courses. We have, of course, included some examples, all from computerised offices. Some of these 'case studies' derive from the authors' own experience, and some from the experience of our delegates. We should like to record our thanks to those organisations whose delegates have provided us with examples. Improbable though some of them may seem, they recount real things which have happened to real people: fiction can never rival fact in the electronic or any other type of office.

As an organisation with over sixty years' experience in supervisory and management training, it was perhaps inevitable that The Industrial Society should take an early lead in teaching the supervisory techniques needed in what is sometimes referred to as 'tomorrow's office'. For many people, this is the office of today, and tomorrow is too long to wait for the guidance and skills necessary to get the best out of both equipment and people.

In keeping with the practical bias of The Industrial Society's courses, our book contains no abstract philosophy. It is an attempt to provide basic, practical and down-to-earth guidelines so that supervisors, whatever their levels of experience, can use the book to help solve some of the problems which the electronic office creates. We felt that it was vital to make the point that supervisors do not need to be 'boffins' if they are to manage an electronic office successfully. The authors have both

come to The Industrial Society's Information
Technology Unit through quite unrelated paths (of
history and biology).

No book can be written without help and support
from others. We should like to thank, firstly, Sue
Smith for her help in typing the manuscript, and
secondly, Chris Wigley for her drawings in Figures
7.1 and 7.2. Finally, we should like to thank our
respective families for their patience and tolerance
during long evenings and weekends spent searching
for just the right words which we hope will make
Supervising the Electronic Office practical, helpful
and easy to read.

Caroline Blaazer

Eric Molyneux

The Industrial Society

The Industrial Society promotes the fullest involvement of all people in their work, in order to increase the effectiveness of organisations and the satisfaction of individuals in creating the goods and services which the community needs.

The Society has over 15,500 member organisations, including industrial and commercial organisations, trades unions, nationalised industries, central and local government departments, employers' organisations and charities. Together they employ over a third of the UK's total labour force. 90 per cent of The Society's revenue is earned from its training and advisory services and 10 per cent from membership subscriptions. It uses this revenue to increase its services to industry, commerce and the public sector.

The Industrial Society was founded in 1918, and is governed by a Council made up of senior managers and trades union officials. It is a totally independent, non-profit making organisation, specialising in practical courses in leadership, communication and consultation, productive management-union relations, conditions of employment and the development of young people at work. Its activities cover the entire UK, and many overseas countries, Holland, Norway and Gibraltar, for example, and many in Africa, the Middle East and the West Indies.

1 Understanding the technology

As a supervisor you need three kinds of expertise in order to do your job effectively:

- technical/professional competence
- administrative ability
- the ability to get the best out of the people in your team.

In this chapter we are concerned mainly with the first feature on our list: technical/professional competence.

In a traditional accounts office, for example, the supervisors need an understanding of accountancy principles and practices in order to be effective. They need to be technically competent in their specialist area of accounts and finance, but they need little or no other technical competence. However, in the electronic office, not only would they need the traditional accounting expertise but they would also be expected to understand the technology that surrounds them. This places an additional responsibility on supervisors which needs to be recognised and accepted. But how detailed does your knowledge of the technology need to be? After all, to continue with the accounts department example, the supervisors are there to manage a team of people producing financial information. They are not there as the experts on the technology being used.

It is nonsensical to suppose that supervisors could survive if they ignored the technological aspects, but to expect the opposite extreme is equally foolish.

The successful route is clearly somewhere in the middle, where the supervisor understands what the technology is expected to achieve and how to use it to its best advantage. This is not such a new idea: many of us do this all the time in our daily lives. How many people completely understand how electricity arrives in our homes? How many people know exactly how a television set works? The answer obviously is that not many people have this knowledge but the vast majority do know how to use their electricity supply and their television set.

So don't worry about being a complete expert on microprocessors and communications technology; it doesn't matter. You should, however, have an understanding in fairly broad terms of what the technology is designed to achieve. After all, as the supervisor you will be ultimately responsible for making sure that the system achieves what is expected.

The following explanations of the various technologies are intended to be simple (some may think them too simple!) and straightforward. We hope that you will find them useful.

BINARY DIGITS

Computer-based systems handle information in the form of binary digits. The simplest way of understanding the binary system used in computing is to compare it with Morse code. The analogy is not perfect but it does provide a basis for understanding.

In Morse code there are two symbols, a dot and a

dash. These dots and dashes can be combined in such a way as to represent letters and numbers. Most people can recognise the S.O.S. message in morse code –

. . . – – – . . .

The binary system also has two symbols, 0 and 1. These two symbols are recognised by computers as a series of on/off electrical pulses. So all the computer system needs to do is to determine between two symbols, off or on, electric current or no electric current. These binary digits are better known as 'bits'.

So all numerals (0–9), letters, punctuation marks and other symbols can be represented by a fixed pattern of bits. With seven binary digits there can be 128 different combinations, ie we can create 128 different characters. This is enough to represent the alphabet twice (once for capital letters and once for lower case) plus numerals and the more common punctuation marks and other symbols used in text. In most cases an eighth digit is added as a check digit, so that we can be told if any of the others are altered by accident. The newest microcomputers are now using 16-bit codes rather than 8-bit since this improves their performance.

HOW A COMPUTER SYSTEM WORKS

Before moving into the intricacies of computerised systems, let us examine how a straightforward manual system operates. A typical process is shown diagrammatically overleaf.

In a manual system the member of staff concerned would receive some form of INPUT (eg a sales order by phone, letter or specialised order form); he or she

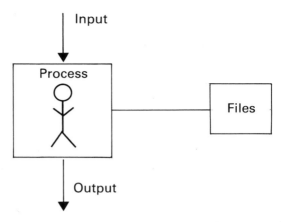

would already have some instructions on how to deal with it. Quite often they would have to refer to appropriate FILES for further information or advice on procedures. They would then PROCESS the order and produce the OUTPUT (eg a works requisition form, an invoice or simply a spoken message on what needs to be done next).

Computerised systems, no matter how sophisticated, operate in essentially the same way as the member of staff described above. There is an INPUT—PROCESS—OUTPUT sequence, very often with reference to FILES.

The most common input device is the keyboard. However, many managers do not possess good keyboard skills and products are now available which use a device called a 'mouse' to allow people to input to the system without using the keyboard.

There are of course many other ways of inputting information and instructions into a computer system. These are the most common:

- voice input
- other devices attached to the computer, called peripherals (punch card readers, cassette tape, floppy discs)

- a transducer (thermocouple, photo-electric cell etc.)
- another computer.

The computer will then 'process' the information according to the instructions it has been given. To do this it may need to read information from other files, which are usually stored on magnetic tape or discs.

Having processed the information the system will produce some form of output. This can be a message on the VDU screen or to some kind of printer attached to the system, or an audible response (sounds, music, words). The output could also go straight to another computer or a display panel. It could be stored on disc, magnetic tape or microfiche.

This basic pattern of INPUT—PROCESS—OUTPUT is always in evidence in the operation of a computerised system. Never forget that if the original input information is rubbish then that is what you will get as output. Put quite simply: 'Garbage in – garbage out'!

WHY THE ELECTRONIC OFFICE?

We have known about binary digits for centuries and computers operating in the way just described have been around for decades. So what has caused the recent developments in what is known generally as information technology? The answer lies in two areas:

- rapid improvements in computer technology, particularly the development of the microprocessor
- significant advances in communications technology.

The convergence of these two technologies has made possible the electronic office.

Why have microprocessors made such an impact?

- They are very small (the newest being no bigger than the size of one letter printed on this page). This means that they are easy to build into all kinds of products, from cars and washing machines to typewriters and microcomputers.
- They are programmable – in other words they can be given instructions to permit them to perform a wide variety of activities. They can also be re-programmed if there is a need to make any changes.
- They can store very large amounts of information. The more advanced microprocessors can store nearly 200,000 individual items of information. That is about the same amount of information as you would find in the telephone directory of a large town.
- Their reliability has been an important feature in their success. With no moving parts they are much less susceptible to failure than any kind of electromechanical device.
- They are cheap, very cheap. If car manufacturers had matched the developments of the microprocessor you could buy a Jaguar car for under £1.00, use it once and throw it away!

What is happening in communications technology?

You may still have problems trying to phone someone in the next street, but the facilities for transmitting data between computers and from computers to their terminals have been improving rapidly. The transmission of data between computers along ordinary telephone lines has been with us for quite a while. In computer terms, though, it has been rather slow and not very reliable. The improvements in this area in recent years will have a significant effect on data transmission. Fibre-optic cables are already being used, the plans to extend and improve the cable television network are in existence, satellites and radio are being used more and more. In the 1980s British Telecom expect to spend £2.5 billion on improvements to their telephone system, particularly in exchanges. The old electromechanical exchanges will disappear, to be replaced by systems controlled by microprocessors. This change will provide faster transmission and a much better chance of making the right connection!

The combination of improved communications facilities and microprocessor technology has caused the 'information revolution'. Add to this the availability of cheap data storage media with very fast access times and the wide variety of reproduction methods and you have the electronic office.

WHAT GOES INTO THE ELECTRONIC OFFICE?

It is extremely difficult to say what hardware is to be found in the electronic office. However, we have included brief descriptions of all the main devices and systems which may be used.

At this point it is worth sounding a warning. You must always remember that the technology is a tool for you to use in your job. Too many supervisors are so fascinated by the technology that they forget what they are supposed to be doing! Do not fall in love with technology; understand it, control it and use it, but always remember that it is only a way of helping you to do your job better.

Word processing

Most organisations make their first move into the electronic office by introducing word processing. Word processors come in all forms, from the smallest memory typewriter through to the most sophisticated models with full A4-size screens and the facility to check common spelling mistakes. However, most systems are essentially 'dedicated microcomputers', in other words they have been designed specifically to handle text. If you have a microcomputer you will be able to buy a word processing package to run on your system. These tend to be slightly more difficult for the operator than the dedicated word processor.

Essentially word processing has three main advantages over traditional typing methods:

- It allows much easier amendment and correction of documents.
- Document storage and retrieval can be much more effective.
- There is much wider variety in the ways in which the document can be printed.

Experience has shown that given good training and guidance most secretarial and typing staff can use word processors quite well. In many organisations the problem lies not with the operator but with the person who originates the work. Too many managers believe that 'you must bung it on the WP' without realising that 'bunging it on the WP' does take time and effort.

Local area networks

Having installed word processors and computers, the most obvious development is to provide a facility which allows them to communicate with each other and with other office systems such as telex, printers, PBX exchange and central data files. This is what a local area network does. It operates on the same principle as a domestic electricity supply: a cable goes around the office building(s) with sockets at various points into which the equipment can be plugged. At the moment a cable similar to television aerial cable is used, but in the future this is likely to be replaced by fibre-optic cable, which will give improved performance, ie more data will be transmitted at higher speeds.

They are called 'local' networks because each covers one building or a group of buildings in close proximity. There are still many difficulties in sending data along wires over long distances which make the speed of communication slow in computer terms. Ordinary telephone lines can cope with approximately 10,000 characters per second, which seems a lot until you compare it with some local area networks that can take 10 million characters per second!

Storing large volumes of information

Most office supervisors are very aware of the problems that can exist with manual, paper-based

filing systems. People have a great capacity for
peculiar methods of filing; files get lost or stored in
the wrong place. It is also a very bulky and expensive
way of keeping information, and many companies
are paying rent and rates for large areas of floor space
occupied by massed ranks of four-drawer filing
cabinets.

The electronic office provides an effective solution
to this kind of problem by allowing electronic
information storage. What it offers is a system which
is small and capable of storing large volumes of
information which can be retrieved very quickly.
Currently the most popular way of achieving this is
the use of magnetic discs. These are thin plastic or
metal discs coated with a substance which allows
them to be magnetised. Information can then be
stored on the disc as a series of magnetic spots which
can be read or written by a read/write head similar to
the head in an ordinary cassette tape player. This
means that any individual item of information can
be 'accessed' in 30–120 milliseconds (a millisecond
is one–thousandth of a second). These magnetic
discs also offer large volumes of storage: over 300
million characters of data.

It is quite likely that even this performance will be
overtaken in coming years with the introduction of
the video data disc. This does not use magnetic
media, but on the surface of each disc there are
millions of tiny indentations. A thin beam of light is
shone on to the disc and reflected back. The
indentations on the disc's surface deflect the beam of
light and this is picked up by the system and
decoded. With this technology one 12″ disc can hold
500 million characters of information on each side.
Because there is no physical contact between the
disc and the disc reader video data discs can operate

much faster and will also last a lot longer than their magnetic counterparts.

Optional extras

The basic elements of the electronic office are personal computing, word processing, local networks and electronic data storage and retrieval. These technologies form the core but other facilities can be included, a few of which merit brief explanations.

Facsimile transmission

Sometimes known as Fax, facsimile transmission is a system which enables copies of a document to be sent along telephone lines and reproduced at the receiving end. This means that diagrams, pictures, maps and so on can be delivered quickly. Fax terminals can transmit one page of A4 in a couple of minutes. Once the refinements to the public telephone network have been completed by British Telecom, this time should come down to something in the region of 15 seconds. At the moment, however, Fax is fairly expensive and suffers from problems in transmission.

Viewdata

Viewdata (or videotext, as it is also known) is a system designed to make large volumes of information (databases) available to people in a relatively simple way. Most viewdata systems use slightly modified television sets which are connected with the central database through public telephone lines. Information is stored in the database as a series of 'frames' or 'pages', with the initial page acting as a

Viewdata is a simple and economical method of providing computer information on an office desk. It uses a modified TV set and the telephone network to enable office staff to consult both private and public data libraries at low cost.

12

'menu' which routes you through the branching system to the page of information you require.

We have covered only a few of the many fascinating technologies that are developing in the office. It would take many volumes to describe them all in detail. Some references for further reading are given at the end of the book.

As a supervisor you must always remember that you will be expected to understand the technology around you. Only by understanding it can you make sure that you manage it and your people effectively.

UNDERSTANDING THE TECHNOLOGY: A SUMMARY

Word processing, facsimile, electronic mail and local area networks are all tools for the job. They are there to do what you the supervisor want them to do. Similarly, your department is your province, not that of the DP department. Understanding the hardware is important only if it helps you to understand the tools of the job and make them work for you, not against you. A clear and total comprehension of the workings of a computer are not essential to the task of the supervisor.

2 Working with the specialists

During the early stages of office automation, whilst the systems are being developed and implemented, it is quite likely that you will be working with various specialists. It is very important during this period that you remember your managerial responsibilities and stay in charge. The specialists will come and go but the office supervisor will remain and will eventually have to make the system produce the goods. Always remember that it is your system (not the computing department's). *Never* abdicate your responsibilities – it is too easy to hand it all over to the specialists and take a back seat yourself. If you do this you will end up with a system which includes the facilities that the specialist thinks you need, which will not be the same as the system which *you* think you need.

HOW TO HANDLE SPECIALISTS

The checklist below forms a sensible basis for a set of ground rules which you should apply when working with specialists.

1   What is his/her name?
2   What is his/her telephone number?
3   Who is his/her boss?
4   What is the boss's telephone number?
5   What are his/her normal hours of work?
6   Do you know when he/she is coming to your department?
7   Does he/she *always* come and see you first before doing anything else in your department?
8   Do you always make the initial introductions to members of your team?
9   Do you know what he/she is doing?
10 Do you know why they are doing it?
11 Do you know what they will do after they have collected the information?

If you are to retain any authority within your department you must know what is going on. Points 8–11 above are vital. You must be able to give your staff reliable information about what the specialist is doing, otherwise the grapevine will take over. Good specialists will always keep you fully informed about what is happening and make sure that you understand. However, if you are unfortunate enough to suffer less than helpful specialists it is up to you to make them tell you what is going on. You must be involved, and be seen by your staff to be involved, if you wish to work effectively with specialists. One of the best ways of ensuring this is to have some understanding of the specialist functions. We refer to the functions rather than the jobs, since in many organisations more than one function may be carried out by the same person.

SYSTEMS ANALYSIS AND DESIGN

Investigation is the first of a series of activities which are commonly known as systems analysis and design and are carried out by someone usually known as a systems analyst. The job title is slightly misleading as analysis is only part of the total function, which has six main activities grouped in two areas.

- Systems investigation
    investigation
    analysis
- Systems design
    design
    communication
    implementation (includes programming)
    monitoring

The investigation and analysis stages are concerned with sorting out what the system will be required to do. This does not really call for a thorough understanding of the intricacies of the computer. The design stage, however, is closely linked with the computer and a detailed knowledge of the capabilities of the computer and associated equipment is required.

Systems investigation

To begin with, the analyst will be asked to investigate the current system and to report back

Teletex is a new, standardised 'protocol' which will allow word processors to send documents to each other throughout Europe, and probably also across the Atlantic. It will act as a kind of 'super telex', but much faster and with many more facilities for the operator.

within a given time. A vital factor in the success of this analysis is the involvement of the staff who have been operating the system under examination. The analyst will rely heavily on you and your staff for the facts he needs. Initially he may conduct a brief survey containing little or no detail, just general information on volume of work, output, frequency of operations etc.

After this initial survey the analyst will discuss his findings with the people involved and then move on to the detailed investigation survey. This survey must be very, very thorough and will take weeks or months to complete. Activities involved in the survey would typically include:

- interviews with you and your staff
- questionnaires on the way in which the work is done
- clarification of facts
- sorting out facts and opinions
- systematic recording of the current ways of working: flow charting, data flow recording, classifying documents
- determining department organisation, manning levels and reporting links
- costing the existing system
- evaluating output from existing systems
- noting shortcomings
- recording exceptional situations
- determining control procedures and necessary security precautions.

During the investigation the analyst is trying to gather as many facts as he can about the way in which your department operates. It is not very helpful if you try to keep things from him in the interests of 'defending' your department. This investigation forms the basis for the development of the computerised system, and if information has been withheld the system will not be effective.

Once all the facts have been gathered during the investigation phase the analysis can start. The analyst will critically examine the system and seek to avoid unnecessary duplication. He will study the reports which are currently produced and determine whether they are necessary and are providing the information needed. It is important to remember that in most organisations the analyst makes suggestions and recommendations but not decisions. After this evaluation and analysis he will be able to determine what the new system should provide. The analyst will present his results to line management and, if his proposals are accepted, the system is then ready for design for the computer and the systems design function takes over.

Systems design

The analyst will have specified the output requirements and will have ascertained how information is put in and which files exist. The designer's job is to relate these to the computer system and to produce the requried output in the most efficient manner. The designer will first of all determine the overall flow of data. This is usually done in flowchart form using the symbols shown below:

Punched card		Magnetic disc	
Keyboard		Printed output	
Punched paper tape		Visual display output	
Operation or process		Graph plotter output	

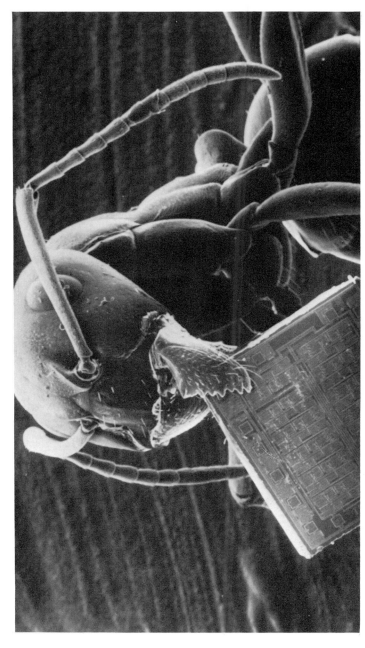

A 'chip' held in the jaws of an ant. The microscopic circuitry on the surface of this component represents the computing power of an entire roomful of data processing equipment of 25 years ago.

The systems designer will then move on to the details, designing forms for source documents, report formats and so on.

As a result of all this a 'system definition' will be produced, containing all the details of the proposed system. This documentation is vital and the supervisor concerned should make sure that they understand it.

Once the system definition is accepted by management work can begin on the computer programs.

COMPUTER PROGRAMMING

A computer program is a list of instructions which will result in the computer system carrying out its required task.

Computer programs are written in a wide variety of languages and it would be impossible for an office supervisor to become completely familiar with them all. Fortunately there is no real need for you to have such a high level of understanding.

The programmer takes the system definition described earlier, expands the procedures described within it and produces logic charts of the system. These logic charts are then checked and if necessary amended by the programmer. He will check the logic in a way designed to detect any logic errors which may be present. Once satisfied that the logic is correct he will carry out the coding into computer language. Again a check is made to make sure that there are no coding errors.

After final testing of the program the programmer will ensure that it is properly documented. This documentation is a most important part of the whole process. The most brilliant piece of programming will be ineffective if it is not documented properly.

COMPUTER OPERATIONS

Once the system is installed it is usually the computer operations section that is responsible for operating it. It is always worthwhile for you to get to know your main contact in the operations section. This is not always possible because large computer operations centres are often on remote sites away from the people they serve. However, if you can possibly arrange it you should go down to the operations room and meet the operations manager and the shift leader. You will find that you get much better service when things go wrong if you know the people you are dealing with.

WORKING WITH THE SPECIALISTS: A SUMMARY

- Always remember that the specialists will come and go. You will be left to get the best out of the system.
- Make sure you know what they are doing in your section.
- Tell your staff about what the specialists are doing — if you don't the grapevine will invent some fairly outrageous stories!
- Work with the specialist not against him. Tell him or her everything you can about the system.
- Make sure that you have some contact, however informal, with the computer operations department.

Case Study: Local Authority

This local authority, like many similar organisations, found itself unable to cope with the increasing volume of paperwork which accompanied the 1974 reorganisation in local government.

The first and most important prerequisite was to enlist the support of the Chief Executive. Without his commitment, the Director, Management and Personnel Services realised that acceptance by staff at all levels would be extremely difficult. An added complication was the presence of a strong union membership whose national policy saw any form of office automation as a direct threat to their membership, and a way of reducing jobs in an area with an already high unemployment rate.

The council's aim was to use word processing not only for regular text processing, and for the annual update of the Register of Electors, but also to try to use the information processing facilities for handling such work as planning applications, standardised instructions for the renovation of council property, records of members of the public holding gun licences, etc. The significance of these data applications was that they were short-term, needing limited storage time and, in the case of gun licences, very small databases.

A six week typing survey was carried out in the Chief Executive's Typing Section to establish workloads and identify potential word processing applications.

The Director, Management and Personnel Services, realised early on that many other local authorities would have similar applications to his own, and spent considerable time in consultation with neighbouring organisations which compared in size with his.

At the suggestion of the Management, the Word Processing Supervisor (designate) and the Word Processing Operators (designate) went on a visit to the offices of a similar organisation, and spent a day chatting to the typists there who had been using word processing for some time. The Typing Services Supervisor was not present, neither was the Organisation Development Officer. This was mainly to ensure that the typists felt totally unfettered and free to comment, try out the keyboards and ask all the questions they wanted. As an exercise in organisation and discipline, the Word

Processing Supervisor (designate) got each typist to write down a list of the questions they would need answered. This exercise, which was extremely successful, played a major part in gaining the commitment of the typists to word processing. Naturally, they also learned a good deal about the way a word processing centre should be run.

From the various visits to other organisations, management drew up a short list of 'preferred' equipment and the final choice was left to the Word Processing Operators following their visits to another authority and two suppliers. A further benefit of the trip to the neighbouring authority was that several members of the typing services staff were union members, and could readily see for themselves that the only parts of their jobs which stood to be altered were those which they had never much liked in the first place. Legal documents such as lease agreements and conveyances came high on this list. The effect, therefore, was effectively to remove any resistance from the unions, who became as enthusiastic about the project as the Organisation Development Officer and the Word Processing Supervisor (designate). By this time, relationships with the unions were such that a regrading exercise was quickly undertaken, which resulted in a separate technician grading being established for the operators, separate from the secretarial and clerical gradings.

One point which the union raised was that of eye tests for staff. The authority agreed that this was highly desirable, and arranged for eye tests to be given by an ophthalmic optician in the town. This gave rise to an interesting situation. When the report arrived from the optician, it stated that all the staff had excellent eyesight, but he was dubious about their ability to reach typing speeds of 500 words per minute. The authority quickly realised that the optician had not clearly understood the nature of the work the typists were going to do, so another test was arranged, at the authority's expense, as the first test had been.

The end result of this careful planning was that the word processor is extremely popular and that new applications are being found for it, by stretching the system to its limits, and sometimes even teaching the suppliers things which they did not know about their own equipment.

One problem remains, and it is a very common difficulty with word processing installations. The authors of text (those who produce the material which is to be done on the word processors) have a somewhat hazy idea of what word processing is and what it does. A programme of author education is still needed, therefore, and the fact that the Organisation Development Officer is aware of this indicates that action is planned to remedy a minor hiccup in a very successful installation.

3 The role of the supervisor

Many supervisors are not sure where they fit within their organisations. Are you part of management or are you 'the first amongst equals' on the office floor? This feeling of being 'the meat in the sandwich' causes great consternation. The Industrial Relations Code of Practice defines a supervisor as a 'member of the first line of management responsible for a work group to a high level of management'. So whether you are called a supervisor, section head, head of department or team leader, if you are in charge of other people you are quite firmly part of the management team. The acceptance of managerial responsibilities at the first level of supervision is an important starting point.

In managing the electronic office there will be many situations which will draw upon your competence as a supervisor. As we saw in Chapter 1, you will need:

- technical competence
- administrative ability
- ability to manage people.

It is quite common to find the largest number of problems under the third heading. Even in the electronic office, where technical expertise and administrative ability have great importance, you will find that the truly effective supervisor is good at averting or dealing with people-problems.

If a supervisor's job is to get people to do things, his success must largely be measured by the ability to get others to work effectively. What do you require to do this? What abilities do you need? You must be in charge of a work group of less than fifteen people so that you can treat the members of the group as individuals and delegate to them effectively; you must enjoy the trust and confidence of the staff, and can begin to do so if you are able to tell them in advance about policies or changes that will affect them; you must ensure that your group is well organised and trained to do the job; you must set up excellent communications with your staff, your colleagues and your boss; most of all you must accept the responsibilities of leadership.

TOOLS TO HELP YOU BECOME MORE EFFECTIVE

The ability to supervise people at work does not just come from books. It comes mainly by practice and experience. However, some of the more painful 'lessons' can be avoided by becoming familiar with some of the supervisor's basic tools.

Getting the work done – a supervisor's checklist

Establish work priorities
1   What is the work objective for this month?
2   What conditions need to exist if this objective
     is to be met?
3   What must I do to ensure that those conditions
     exist?

Make contingency plans
4   What could happen to prevent me achieving
     my objective?
5   Which of these are most likely to happen?
     (identify no more than four)
6   What must be done to prevent those things
     most likely to happen from happening?
7   If they do happen what is my plan for handling
     each situation?

Monitor progress
8   What points must I check/visit during each
     working period?
9   What is the best time (if any) to check/visit
     each point?
10   What is the longest time I can reasonably allow
     an error at each point to go unchecked?
11   Considering all information above, what must
     my route and timing be for 'walking the job'?

Review and evaluate
12   When should I review progress towards my
     objectives – daily, weekly, monthly? (fix the
     date and duration of the session in your diary
     and stick to it)

Knowing the procedures

There is more to good supervision than the unthinking application of rules and procedures. However, it is vital that you know what procedures cover your staff and that you understand their implications for your work. The following checklist might help:

Have I a copy of:	Yes/No	If no, where can it be found?	Date read and understood

Grievance procedure
Disciplinary procedure
Appeals procedure
Company rules
Company contract of
    employment form
Sick pay scheme
Company safety policy
Trade union recognition
    agreement
Redundancy agreement
Bonus/incentive scheme			

Others			

Some statistics to help you monitor your own performance

Be careful when using statistics and remember the phrase about lies, damned lies and statistics! The figures overleaf are only helpful when compared with figures produced in the same manner from a similar source.

PEOPLE

Absence

$$\frac{\text{Total days lost through absence}}{\text{Average number of employees}}$$ = Average number of days lost per employee over period covered

$$\frac{\text{Total number of hours/shifts/days lost} \times 100}{\text{Total planned hours/shifts/days}}$$ = Hours/shifts/days lost as percentage oɪ planned working time

Labour turnover

$$\frac{\text{Number of leavers per month} \times 12 \times 100}{\text{Average number of employees during year}}$$ = Monthly labour turnover figure expressed as an annual percentage

PRODUCTIVITY/EFFICIENCY

Materials

$$\frac{\text{Total rejects per batch/period} \times 100}{\text{Total output (including rejects)}}$$ = Reject rate

$$\frac{\text{Total output of acceptable quality} \times 100}{\text{Total material used throughout manufacturing process}}$$ = Material recovery rate

Machines

$$\frac{\text{Actual machine running time} \times 100}{\text{Available machine time}} \quad = \text{Machine utilisation}$$

$$\frac{\text{Actual machine production rate} \times 100}{\text{Planned machine production rate}} \quad = \text{Machine efficiency}$$

Labour

$$\frac{\text{Total man-hours spent on production} \times 100}{\text{Total man-hours available}} \quad = \text{Labour utilisation}$$

Accidents

$$\frac{\text{Number of lost-time}^* \text{ accidents} \times 100}{\text{Total man-hours worked}} \quad = \text{Frequency rate}$$

*A lost-time accident is one which prevents the injured person from continuing his normal job beyond the day or shift on which the accident occurred. Transfers to alternative work are, therefore, included in the statistics.

$$\frac{\text{Total man-hours lost (excl. fatalities)}}{\substack{\text{Total number of lost-time accidents} \\ \text{(excl. fatalities)}}} \quad \begin{array}{l} = \text{Duration rate} \\ \text{(average hours} \\ \text{spent away from job} \\ \text{by injured person)} \end{array}$$

Suggestions

$$\frac{\text{Total suggestions submitted} \times 100}{\text{Average number of employees}} \quad \begin{array}{l} = \text{Submission rate per} \\ \text{100 employees} \end{array}$$

$$\frac{\text{Total accepted suggestions} \times 100}{\text{Average number of employees}} \quad \begin{array}{l} = \text{Acceptance rate per} \\ \text{100 employees} \end{array}$$

THE SUPERVISOR'S LEADERSHIP ROLE

The ability to get people to give of their best to their work is an important skill for all supervisors. The 'novelty' of the electronic office soon disappears and you cannot rely on the technology to keep people going! Any supervisor is first and foremost the leader of a work group and acceptance of this leadership role is vital in achieving supervisory success.

Leadership qualities

When asked the question 'What makes an effective leader?', most people would produce a list of personal qualities similar to the one below:

- judgement
- initiative
- integrity
- honesty
- fairness
- dedication
- ambition
- decisiveness
- dependability
- approachability
- tenacity.

The problem with producing such a list is knowing when to stop! How many qualities are we looking for? Should there be 8 or 80? Which is the most important? Most of these qualities are also matters of personal judgement and cannot be closely defined or measured. Someone that you regard as tenacious may well be viewed by someone else as obstinate and pigheaded!

Whilst any group will expect its leader to possess certain qualities, there is no perfect mix for all given situations. Perhaps the greatest weakness in concentrating too much on qualities is that they are not easily taught. How can a supervisor be trained to be honest and dedicated? There is no evidence to suggest that if people listen to lectures on integrity they absorb something of that quality into themselves. Leadership qualities are important but they are not the whole story.

The situational approach

There is a body of opinion which believes that it is not the qualities of the leader that are important, but the situation in which leaders find themselves. It is argued that as each different situation requires different leadership skills the person with the most appropriate skills will emerge as the work group leader for that situation. For example, if a group of people witnessed a road accident, any doctor, nurse or trained first-aider in the group would assume the leadership of the group.

This concept of constantly changing leadership makes a fascinating theory but has never been proved to work successfully in most offices. At work we have a structure: you are the office supervisor today, tomorrow, next week, next month. You are there to deal with all the different situations that arise. The practice of changing the leadership every time there is a new situation to manage simply causes confusion and misunderstanding.

The functional approach

The most successful method of developing leadership skills has been found to be the approach which concentrates on the 'functions' of leadership, ie what leaders actually *do* rather than what they *are*.

This approach has become known as Action-Centred Leadership (ACL) because it concentrates on the actions that the leader takes.

There are three main areas in which leaders need to take action. They need to

- achieve the task
- build the team
- develop individuals.

Because each of these areas has an effect on the others they are best shown diagrammatically as three overlapping circles.

You must ensure that the required tasks and jobs are completed, while at the same time supervising your group in such a way that the group work and group identity are maintained and developed. You must also recognise that each person who makes up the team is an individual with needs, hopes and ideas which must be fulfilled if the individual is to be effective. If a supervisor pays too much attention to achieving the task at whatever the cost, sooner or later the team will begin to disintegrate. Similarly, if by ignoring individual needs a supervisor fails to spot the rotten apple, very soon there will be a rotten barrel. The performance of the team will suffer and the team may indeed disintegrate. The three-circle model above indicates that the effective leader must work at all three areas if a high level of performance is to be sustained.

Achieving the task

You must:

1 Have a clear idea about what the task is.
2 Understand how the task fits into the objectives of the company.
3 Plan how the task will be accomplished.
4 Define and provide the resources you need, ie time, authority, equipment, staff and so on.
5 Ensure that the organisational structure allows the task to be achieved effectively.
6 Control progress.
7 Evaluate the results.

Building the team

The difference between a collection of individuals and a cohesive group or team is that in a team the individuals are willing and able to work together – to co-operate. They can do this when they are made aware of their common purpose. Individuals in work groups often have different and separate tasks, not common tasks, but these individual tasks invariably have a common purpose. It is the leader's job to make them aware of what it is, in order to win their co-operation. Here is a short checklist to help you build and maintain your team:

Digital Optical Recording, a Philips invention, allows a single, 12-inch disk like this to store half a million pages of typewritten text, and to display any one within a few seconds. This system could become the office filing cabinet of the future.

1   Get them together regularly in order to
    (a)   brief them about objectives and their
          achievement – 'what we are trying to
          achieve and how we are doing'
    (b)   consult them for their ideas, opinions,
          suggestions for improvement.
2   Talk about 'we' instead of 'I'.
3   Help to resolve conflicts when they occur.
4   Speak up for the team when necessary.
5   Organise the team to make the widest use of
    individual talents.
6   Establish common standards and stick to them.

It follows that if you involve your team in determining objectives, in choosing working methods, in reorganising work schedules, in solving problems, in making decisions, you will have them behind you and will be better able to change team practices than if you give separate instructions to each individual member or impose new orders and instructions. By involving the team you will be more effective in bringing about support for needed change and better implementation of the new technologies in the office.

Developing individuals

To bring out the best in an individual you must have some knowledge about what makes that person 'tick', particularly what makes him 'tick' at work, so that he can be motivated to give better and more productive work.

People work for many reasons: to attain high levels of material comfort, for recognition and prestige, for social service and for the work itself, if it is sufficiently interesting and challenging. There are probably many other reasons, but the real problem lies in trying to decide why people do *not* work as hard as they could. There have been many surveys on this question and broadly speaking the results can be categorised under these headings:

- bad working conditions
- fear: of redundancy, changes, inadequacy etc.
- boredom
- personal worries
- poor supervision
- feeling of unimportance
- lack of incentive
- poor relationships with colleagues
- lack of information about the job and surroundings.

You can probably add to the following list of suggestions for positive action the supervisor can take to lift people from minimal performance to efficient, effective production.

1 Help staff to realise that work can be a satisfying integral part of life itself.
2 Provide clear targets by which their performance can be measured.
3 Consider any incentives, financial and otherwise.
4 Give praise where praise is due and be specific.
5 Keep people informed of any changes, so that they have a sense of security.
6 Respect your staff as individuals.

7 Involve staff in the overall job so that their interest is developed.

8 Keep a close eye on working conditions. Notice defects and put forward recommendations for improvements.

9 Be constantly on the lookout for improved layouts and methods.

To provide the right atmosphere and opportunities for each individual to achieve satisfaction and self-fulfilment is probably the most difficult area of the leader's job, but if successful it can also be the most rewarding.

The three checklists on pp. 40–43 supplement this discussion and provide a useful reference for the future.

HANDLING EVERYDAY SITUATIONS

Being on the first level of management you will often find yourself the first person to come across awkward situations and staff problems. It is important that you know how to deal with these situations effectively. Nobody respects a supervisor who is constantly pushing things upwards to the boss. We have already mentioned the importance of making yourself familiar with the procedures which exist within your organisation. You should know exactly where your authority starts and where it ends. There is nothing more embarrassing than having one of your decisions overturned by your boss because you failed to follow correct procedure or overstepped your authority.

The following sections on disciplinary action, dealing with a grievance, conducting counselling

ACTIONS BY LEADERS

1   Set the task of the team; put it across with
    enthusiasm and remind people of it often.

2   Make leaders accountable for 4–15 people; instruct
    them in leadership actions.

3   Plan the work, check its progress, design jobs and
    arrange work to encourage the commitment of
    individuals and the team.

4   Set individual targets after consulting; discuss
    progress with each person regularly, but at least
    once a year.

5   Delegate decisions to individuals. If not, consult
    those affected before you decide.

6   Communicate the importance of everyone's job;
    explain decisions to help people apply them; brief
    team together monthly on progress, policy, people,
    and points for action.

7   Train and develop people, especially the young;
    gain support for the rules and procedures, set an
    example and 'have a go at' those who break them.

8   Where unions are recognised, encourage joining,
    attendance at meetings, standing for office and
    speaking up for what each person believes is in the
    interest of the organisation and all who work in it.

9   Serve people in the team and care for their
    wellbeing; improve working conditions and safety;
    work alongside people; deal with grievances
    promptly and attend social functions.

10 Monitor action: learn from successes and mistakes;
    regularly walk round each person's place of work,
    observe, listen and praise.

ACTION-CENTRED LEADERSHIP: KEY ACTIONS

Key actions	Task	Team	Individual
Define objectives.	Identify task and constraints.	Involve team. Share commitment.	Clarify objectives. Gain acceptance.
Plan.	Establish priorities. Check resources. Decide. Set standards.	Consult. Encourage ideas and actions. Develop suggestions. Structure.	Assess skills. Set targets. Delegate.
Brief.	Brief the team. Check understanding.	Answer questions. Obtain feedback.	Listen. Enthuse.
Support. Monitor.	Report progress. Maintain standards. Discipline.	Co-ordinate. Reconcile conflict.	Advise. Assist/reassure. Recognise effort. Counsel.
Evaluate.	Summarise progress. Review objectives. Replan if necessary.	Recognise success. Learn from failure.	Assess performance. Appraise. Guide and train.

ACTION-CENTRED LEADERSHIP – THREE CIRCLES

Task:

Purpose:	Am I clear what the task is?
Responsibilities:	Am I clear in what mine are?
Objectives:	Have I agreed these with my boss for the group?
Programme:	Have I worked one out to reach objectives?
Working conditions:	Are these right for the job?
Resources:	Are these adequate (authority, money, materials)?
Targets:	Has each member clearly defined and agreed them?
The boss:	Does everyone know to whom he/she is accountable?
Group size:	Is this too large – can it be made smaller (4–18)?
Authority:	Is the line of authority clear?
Training:	Are there any gaps in the group's abilities?
Priorities:	Have I planned the time?
Progress:	Do I check this regularly and evaluate?
Supervision:	In case of absence who covers?
Example:	Do I set standards by my behaviour?
	Do I visit people at their work?

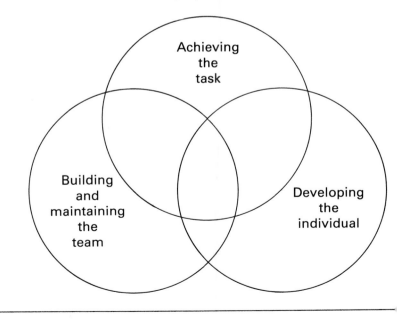

Achieving the task

Building and maintaining the team

Developing the individual

Team members:

Objectives:	Does the team understand them?
Standards:	Do they know what is expected?
Quality:	What standards are acceptable?
Safety:	Do they know consequences of infringement?
Size of team:	Is the number correct?
Team members:	Are the right people working together?
Team spirit:	Is the job structured to encourage this?
Discipline:	Are the rules seen to be reasonable? Am I impartial?
Grievances:	Are these dealt with promptly? Is there a formal procedure?
Consultation:	Is this genuine? Do I encourage and welcome ideas and suggestions?
Briefing:	Is this regular?
Trade unions:	Do the team know the organisation's attitude?
Group representatives:	ie shop stewards etc. Do they have the facilities to be effective?
Back-up:	Am I prepared to represent the feelings of the group when required? Do I visit people at their work?

Individual:

Targets:	Have they been agreed and quantified?
Induction:	Does he/she really know the organisation?
Achievement:	Does he/she know his/her work contribution?
Responsibilities:	Has he/she got a job description?
Authority:	Does he/she have sufficient for task?
Training:	Has adequate provision been made?
Recognition:	Do I emphasise people's successes? In failure is criticism constructive?
Growth:	Does he/she see the chance of development?
Performance:	Is this regularly reviewed?
Reward:	Are work capacity and pay in balance?
The task:	Is he/she in the right job?
The person:	Do I know the person well?
Time/attention:	Do I spend enough with individuals listening, developing, counselling?
Grievances:	Are these dealt with promptly?
Security:	Does he/she know about pensions, redundancy etc.? Do I visit people at their work?

interviews and taking decisions present the main
elements that you should be aware of.

Taking disciplinary action

Remember:

- the purpose of disciplinary action is to
  correct behaviour or improve performance,
- you must wherever possible identify and
  treat the cause of disciplinary failures, not
  just the effect.

1 Identify the issue.
   - Has an offence been committed?
   - What are the rules and standards
     expected?
   - Do not pre-judge the actions of others.
2 Confront the individual(s) concerned.
   - Inform of breaches of discipline or
     standards of work.
   - Ask 'why': get an explanation for
     behaviour.
   - Check whether individual(s) concerned
     knew the rules and standards expected.
   - Listen; observe; note main points.
   - If the incident is serious misconduct
     isolate the individual or suspend on full
     pay pending further investigation.
3 Investigate.
   - Check the facts gathered so far.
   - Consult records, rules and procedures,
     personal files, other people who can help
     or advise.

4   Decide on your approach.
- What offence has been committed (precision)?
- Was the behaviour/action justified in the circumstances (consider cause and effect)?
- Should action be taken to: a) remove the cause? b) penalise behaviour? c) both?
- What course of action is proposed to be taken – is it beyond your level of authority?
- How should it be presented to those involved to gain acceptance and retain co-operation?
- What reaction can be expected – how will you handle it?
- When and where will you interview the individual(s) concerned?

5   Conduct a disciplinary interview.
- Be firm but understanding.
- Advise of and establish the offence (be specific).
- Indicate the possible consequences.
- Allow individual(s) the right to be represented.
- Give individual(s) the chance to state case formally.
- Keep calm; do not argue or use bad language.
- Listen; observe; take notes.
- Ask questions to gain full understanding.
- Summarise.
- If possible get the individual(s) to suggest a course of action in the light of the conversation so far.

6   Take final decision.
- Reconsider initial decision on possible

action to be taken; amend where
necessary; announce your final decision.
- If uncertain refer situation to another
party and state date/time final decision
will be announced.
- Inform of procedure by which to appeal
against decision.

7   Follow up on agreed action.
- Record the interview and action to be
taken by all parties.
- Confirm to all parties agreed action in
writing.
- Check future behaviour, attitude,
performance.
- See that necessary help is given if
required and check with person(s)
concerned.
- Praise and encourage improvements.
- Check that warnings etc. are removed
from personal files in line with company
procedure.

Dealing with a grievance

1   Listen to the grievance.
- Be sympathetic; show concern.
- Write down the main points.
- Ask questions and summarise to
establish the circumstances causing
dissatisfaction.
- If possible get individual to suggest a
solution.
- Do not commit yourself too quickly.

2   Investigate.
- Check the facts, eg names, dates, times,

        places, attitudes, etc.
- Clarify personal circumstances, health, work record, domestic situation (where appropriate).
- Review company rules, procedures, policy, custom and practice.

3 Assess the facts.
- Establish the pros and cons.
- Look at precedents (if any).
- Is there a genuine case for action?
- Can you handle the grievance or should you pass it to a higher authority for action?
- How much time have you left in which to decide action?

4 Decide.
- What you are going to do to remove dissatisfaction.
- Anticipate reaction and have answers ready.
- Write down how you will put your decision across.
- If in doubt consult with the person at the next stage in the grievance procedure.

5 Communicate what you propose to do.
- Arrange to meet the individual.
- Invite their representative to be present if appropriate.
- Ensure privacy and no interruptions.
- If no decision has been reached or proposed action is unacceptable, state nature of future action or the procedure for an appeal.

6 Follow up.
- Check that what was agreed should happen has happened.
- Are relationships, attitudes, performance acceptable?

Conducting a counselling interview

1 Purpose
   To discuss and advise on problems affecting
   a person's work with the object of solving or
   alleviating the problem, bearing in mind the
   needs of both the employer and the individual
2 Preparation
   ● plan approach according to individual
   ● ensure privacy
   ● allow adequate time
   ● check details and addresses of specialists
     who could help:
       Citizens Advice Bureau
       Local authority (social services)
       Marriage guidance counsellor
   ● check file on individual
3 Conduct
   ● put at ease
   ● guide interviewee to finding out solution
   ● listen carefully
   ● be sensitive and understanding
   ● establish problem clearly
   ● come to a positive conclusion with
     positive ideas and points for action
4 Follow up
   ● arrange for future interview to check
     developments
   ● carry out any action promised

Taking decisions

Taking a decision will be influenced primarily by
these factors:

   ● the severity of the situation

- the degree of urgency
- the degree of authority within which to act
- the effect of the decision on others.

Decision-taking has to be approached in a systematic way so as to promote greater consistency and efficiency. Experience shows that there are five main actions supervisors need to take, and take instinctively. They are known as the five Cs of decision-taking:

1 CONSIDER – the preparation stage at which you consider the problem

2 CONSULT – the stage at which you take initiatives to involve those affected

3 CRUNCH – the point at which you do something about it

4 COMMUNICATE – the stage at which you explain what has been decided and why

5 CHECK – the process of going back and making sure the decision actually works

These five words imply, of course, that at every stage a number of other actions have to receive consideration as well. The following framework suggests what some of those actions might be:

CONSIDER	CONSULT	CRUNCH	COMMUNICATE	CHECK
Clarify problem. Check for cause or effect. Make sure it is your decision to take.	Make maximum amount of information available.	Gather all the options.	Brief what will happen, why, and whom the decision affects.	Check that briefing is carried out.
Clarify ultimate objectives and time and other constraints.	Call a meeting of those involved or their representatives.	TAKE THE DECISION.	Back up briefing with written confirmation of the decision.	Run spot checks to monitor effectiveness.
Ask yourself, and others, what information you need.	Decide at which stage the consultation will stop; make clear right of appeal.	Write down the implementation plan.	Make sure everyone understands when the decision will be implemented.	Review decision and take any necessary corrective action.

INDUCTION OF NEW STAFF

First impressions can last a long, long time and when new staff join your department you want to make sure that their first impression is favourable. The induction of new starters is something which should never be delegated. Other people will of course be involved in the induction process, but you must remain accountable for making sure that everything happens. It is your opportunity to get off to a good start with new employees and the following checklist contains some useful advice from generally accepted practices:

Departmental information
Given by supervisor on receiving new employee
    What the department makes or does
    Where it fits in the company
    Jobs
    Organisation
    Supervisors' names
    Other employees
    Representatives
    Department rules
    Breaks: tea, meals, union
    Where the job fits into the department
    Mobile or dangerous equipment

Services and amenities
Given by colleague during departmental tour on first day
    First aid, medical facilities, union
    Canteen
    Toilets
    Overalls/protective clothing

Personal relationships
Given by supervisor at end of first day
    Help and co-operation $\begin{cases} \text{You from them} \\ \text{Them from you} \end{cases}$
    Requests
    Time off
    Promotion

Discipline
Given by supervisor during second day
    Absence
    Lateness
    Smoking
    Co-operation
    Discipline procedure
    Expectations $\begin{cases} \text{You from them} \\ \text{Them from you} \end{cases}$

Standards
Given by supervisor during third day
    Efficiency
    Quality
    Safety/accident procedure
    Good housekeeping
    Hygiene
    Security arrangements

Pay and hours
Given by supervisor before first payday
    Hours: overtime
           weekends
           shifts
    Clocking on/off
    Bonus cards
    Pay point and procedure

Miscellaneous
Given by supervisor at end of second week
  Fire precautions/procedure
  Trade union membership
  Grievance procedure
  Suggestion scheme

At the end of the first month of employment hold an interview to check that the employee knows the following information:

Company information
  Name
  History
  Products/services
  Location of head office
  Managers' names

Pay and hours
  Rates: deductions
             queries
  Pay: where/how/when
             loans
  Bonus: production
             annual
  Pension scheme: deductions
  Pay slip: explain
  Sickness: notification
             certification
             pay
  Notice: period
  Holiday: statutory
             annual
  Contract of employment

Miscellaneous
  Sports/social clubs etc.
  Travelling
  Further education/training

ORGANISING YOURSELF

In order to carry out effectively the supervisory part of your job it is important that you organise yourself properly. A significant amount of time and effort can be saved by some fairly simple actions. You will find that good leadership takes time, therefore you have to make sure that you have the time to give by organising yourself in the most efficient manner possible. One of the most important things you can do is to learn to delegate, not just 'bitsy' jobs but significant chunks of your everyday work. This has great advantages not only in giving you valuable time but because of its generally positive influence on the development of the individual to whom you have delegated.

Be particularly careful when dealing with 'paperwork', even if it does appear as a screen of information on a VDU. Electronic mail can be just as time-consuming to deal with as the old-fashioned paper stuff! Don't just plough through it – you need to have some system for organising priorities and getting the most important actions taken. A colleague of ours has a desk drawer labelled OBE, which has nothing to do with the honours list. In that drawer he puts everything which he believes will be Overtaken By Events! Most of us do not need to take such drastic measures, but you must develop for your own use some system of sorting out the 'important' from the 'urgent'. The following suggestion may be a helpful starting point.

Write down your jobs under such headings as:

● training
● checking completed work
● liaising with other departments.

Rearrange the list so that the functions appear in order of importance and put beside each function an estimate of the amount of time it takes every week. Then ask yourself these questions:

- Am I spending enough time on the more important matters?
- Can I reduce the time spent on the less important matters?
- Can I delegate any jobs?
- Are all the jobs still relevant or can some be eliminated?
- Have I left any time for 'nothing in particular'?

Once you have sorted out your priorities it is possible to work out a rough programme of day-to-day activities. Some jobs must be done daily, some weekly, some at longer intervals. You need to develop a simple system to ensure that nothing is overlooked.

PRESENTING A CASE TO MANAGEMENT

From time to time you may be called upon to present to higher management your views, feelings or knowledge. It is important that you put your message across as effectively as you can. This takes time and effort. Never think that you can simply walk in and 'play it by ear'. You should always aim to be:

- objective
- short and to the point
- positive in what you want to say.

Effective speaking comes with practice and preparation but you can gain a lot by following the three stages shown below:

Stage 1: Preparation
Your purpose: what is your objective?
Your subject: know your facts/collect useful examples.
Your listeners: know your audience – their attitudes, present knowledge, capacity.
Your time limit: how long have you got?

Stage 2: Shape of talk
State your proposition: state subject, arouse interest, show enthusiasm.
Face the snags: weigh up what is against you, concede flaws graciously, anticipate objections.
Prove your case: select and highlight strong points.
Summary: re-state main points, finish on conclusive note.

Stage 3: Delivery
Be natural: no affected voice, distracting mannerisms.
Be confident: know your subject, do not show nervousness.
Show your evidence: illustrate your facts with examples.
Be enthusiastic: show that you are keen on your subject.
Be friendly: like your audience.

THE ROLE OF THE SUPERVISOR: A SUMMARY

As a member of the management team, the supervisor needs a set of clear, simple guidelines to help get the job done.

Good results do not just come from leaders who are objective or dependable: they result from the things that leaders do to pay attention to individuals, to create and maintain team spirit and to get the task achieved. The actions that a good leader can and must take are totally within the competence of every single one of us.

Case Study: Heavy Engineering Plant, West Midlands

This company decided in May 1983 to try to shift its computerisation operation from the specialist DP department to the wider user area in the office. They hoped to benefit from the experiences of other organisations, and felt that this decentralisation of the DP function would benefit the company. It is an important element of the company ethos that staff should all enjoy their work, and that everyone should have a chance to benefit from learning about new office technology, if they had the aptitude and interest. A Central Services Department was planned to consist of 11 jobs, which would cover the following areas:

- telephone exchange and reception/telex
- typing/administration
- customer services
- accurate technical documentation on projects
- accounts receivable
- invoices
- elementary figure work

At a regular monthly Board meeting, the Managing Director outlined the plan which was to be fully implemented by Christmas. An Organisation and Study sub-committee was set up, one of whose key members was the Systems Administration Manager, whose responsibility included setting up the new scheme. The sub-committee's second meeting received an unexpected directive from the Managing Director that there were to be 200 redundancies in other parts of the plant.

The sub-committee reported to the Board on its findings and made recommendations but the report was poorly received, mainly because the managers objected strenuously to the prospect of losing their secretaries. They pointed out that they needed a great deal of work typed and that the Central Services Department could in no way cope with this, as well as the day-to-day administration work done by the secretaries.

The Managing Director then made two decisions:

1 that a word processing pool would be set up, and

2 that individual directors would announce the redundancies to their respective departments.

The Systems Administration Manager meantime lost his place on the sub-committee and, from then on, lost touch with the progress of the project. In terms of staff numbers, 19 people were involved, and there were only jobs for 11. Individual letters were sent to all the staff immediately concerned, inviting them to individual half-hour interviews to try to assess their aptitude and interest in joining the new department. The interviews were held by the Personnel Director, with the Systems Administration Manager present. Because the staff hardly knew the Personnel Director, they found it difficult to communicate effectively with him. Since the Systems Administration Manager was no longer a part of the sub-committee, he had lost credibility in the view of the staff. For these reasons, the interviews were not considered an unqualified success.

Meanwhile, equipment had been ordered, including three word processors, and the secretaries who were to work in the new department moved down to their new locations. They were assured that they would still be secretaries, and that they could still carry out their PA duties for their bosses. The distance between the new department and the bosses' offices, however, made this impracticable. In the new department, an informal hierarchy grew up, with the (ex) secretaries at the top of the pyramid and marked divisions in departmental relationships.

The situation worsened when a vacancy arose for an assistant to one of the executives. Although this was emphatically stated not to be a secretarial post, two of the secretaries applied for the position but were unsuccessful. Another candidate was appointed, but mistrust increased because the secretaries had been told that there would be no secretarial posts. They found it difficult to believe the management explanation of the situation, and began to feel that there was one rule for them and another for everyone else.

By this time, a supervisor had been appointed to the new department. He had had supervisor experience within the company, but was also known to be a fairly strict disciplinarian. Morale sank even further. Other problems began to show themselves. There had been no receptionist training. The lady in the post room was told to smile and look pleasant, but nothing more. The telex was situated beside the receptionist's desk, so the receptionist was constantly interrupted from telex work by the flow of visitors one would normally expect in a large international organisation.

The secretaries, unaccustomed to formal supervision such as they now found, were not working to capacity because they were not carrying out the administrative, telephone and message-carrying duties they used to do for their managers. One of the main objections of their managers had been the volume of typing which needed to be done. On the day when the office was visited, six pieces of work were in the IN basket waiting for attention, each averaging four pages, and some had been there since the previous day. During the third week of September, and after the relocation of the staff in the new department, the word processors arrived. They were placed on the floor of the office where they would be used. There was no furniture, one radiator and no windows except glass wall-panels painted white. The only ventilation was an 8" extractor fan. The Health and Safety Officer had already stated that the lighting (fluorescent) was inadequate.

The present situation is:

- several secretaries are applying for other jobs, in and outside the company
- the prevailing atmosphere can best be described as 'chilly'.

Conclusion: A great deal of painstaking bridge-building needs to be done, unless the company can wait for the currently disaffected staff to leave, and can start afresh with personnel who are untainted by the events which led up to the present situation.

4 Managing change at work

A great many people seem to see change at work in a totally negative light. Change is 'bad', 'dangerous', 'harmful' and 'threatening'. It is characteristic of offices that they have, until the late 'seventies, relied on virtually the same procedures and methods as they did a century ago. Voice input and output by telephone, data/text capture by shorthand or tape media, reproduction of that data/text on a typewriter, paper files: none of these has changed in its essentials during the lifetime of most people at work today. It is hardly surprising, therefore, that the sudden and rapid change in office procedures has caused so much interest and aroused so much anxiety, not to mention antagonism.

Without our necessarily realising it, change is in fact a normal part of our everyday lives. You may have had a visit from a retired employee, who has looked around and commented that things have changed a lot since his or her time. 'And a good thing, too', you might mentally retort. Any organisation which is too rigid in its structure and outlook and refuses to adapt to new techniques and equipment runs a severe risk of falling badly behind the competition. The British economy is full of such examples, the motor cycle industry to name but one.

Overseas, one could cast a glance at the Swiss watch industry, which has been crippled by the digital watch.

Organisations are almost always in a state of change to some degree. Like amoebae, nuclei form, change shape, are split or broken off, join up with others or disappear altogether. Changes of this type are caused by boardroom shuffles, takeovers, new product developments, legislation, political factors, public opinion: the list is endless.

One of the main reasons why the electronic revolution has caused such an upheaval is that it has been very expensive. The low level of investment in offices over the last twenty or more years has sharpened the impact of the current injections of millions of pounds' worth of electronic gadgetry. In some offices the change is so radical as to leap from manual typewriters to computers, word processors and screen-based telex and laser printers.

A second reason is that it is quite apparent that this is only a prelude to even greater changes, which promise to be even more complex and expensive. This has caused some managements to exercise undue caution, preventing them from investing in automated products because they know they will be superseded in a year or two. This view of things is short-sighted and is analogous to someone with an inadequate car holding back from buying a new one because next year's models may have larger boots or better fog lamps.

Finally, electronic change in the office is perceived as a threat because it automates some basic office functions, especially the capture, reproduction, storage and retrieval of data and text.

For too long people in offices have seen their jobs as ends in themselves, rather than as the means by which the company achieves certain objectives. As a

A typical office micro-computer system. The workstation is small and unobtrusive, while the central processor (on the left) and the printer can be positioned anywhere convenient. This system allows several users to share the same printer and processor.

result, when the systems analysts or the O and M
department, notepads in hand, are trying to design
workable automated systems they find themselves
face to face with managers who have long since
forgotten why they need ten copies of this document
and six of another. These managers often cannot
explain why the accounts department needs the blue
sheets: in a word, managers and supervisors find
themselves unable to explain and articulate the
objectives of their departments or sections.

ˊ Because of this, managers and supervisors feel that
they are starting at a disadvantage, particularly as
they find much of the technology difficult to
understand. They are often nervous of the skills and
language of the data processing department and
resign themselves to being told what to do without
having the assertiveness to tell the analysts what
they need to achieve in their own work areas.

FEAR OF CHANGE

The fear of change at work can have many causes,
some of them very deep-seated, and the supervisor
will do well to recognise and understand them. In
this section we look at the most common of these
causes and consider ways in which the supervisor
can attempt to deal with them.

Inability to learn new equipment

The need to learn new equipment causes more panic
than any other single factor in people whose offices
are undergoing change. Supervisors generally want

An executive workstation. This desk-top device, usually comprising just a screen and a keyboard, enables managers to consult and use their company's central computer facility. The computer is fast enough to share out its services amongst very large numbers of individual users.

to feel that they understand the new systems better than their subordinates, and readily recognise their responsibility to learn as much as they can. Often, however, they will not be in the first flush of youth and will find the learning process slow and frustrating. If they are male, this situation may often be aggravated by a feeling that keyboarding work is not a job which men ought to do. If the supervisors are men promoted from the shop floor, they will probably consider keyboard-type work to be effete and somewhat beneath their dignity.

In any event, the greatest challenge you face as a supervisor in this situation is to learn better and faster than your staff who may be younger than you and who are, for this reason, more receptive to new ideas. Younger staff will also be nearer to the formal learning days of their schooling than most supervisors.

Added to this is the likelihood that your learning may have to take place in an open plan office where people may be able to see you making embarrassing mistakes. If you try to take the easy way out by not bothering to learn the new equipment, you run a severe risk of losing credibility with your staff, to say nothing of the difficulties of discussing matters of departmental policy with specialist programmers and analysts if you are starting from a weak base.

Supervisors apart, staff may themselves feel anxious that they will not be able to master the new equipment. This fear will be especially marked among staff in the 40-plus age bracket, because of their fear that they may be outstripped by much younger staff who are subordinate to them both in age and service with the company. The commonest reaction to this fear is the argument that the old system was perfectly adequate and that they can see no good reason to change it.

Loss of status

People earn status, or are accorded status by others, for a variety of reasons. They may hold a position of seniority in terms of long service, or they may be the person who normally trains new recruits to do their jobs. Within a working department, subsections may form themselves without the supervisor always being aware of it. When these informal subgroups appear, one member may assume an informal leadership role by virtue of age, force of personality or experience. When an entire department is to be converted to working on VDU terminals, this structure, informal though it may be, is placed under threat and people who have held superior positions in the informal pecking order may lose these positions and the status associated with them.

Everyone in the department may be lumped together regardless of former status, formal or otherwise, to learn the new equipment. This is bound to cause some resentment. Older staff may fear that they will not be 'picked' to operate new equipment and this will diminish their status as well. Status at work can also stem from being the person who, for example, checks information, signs sanctions or handles certain types of queries. If this chain of action is altered by computerisation of the office, the status associated with the activity involved will also disappear.

When change is in the air, people do not often stop to think that, for every status-laden job which disappears, a new job may surface with equal, or greater, status. It is even less likely that people will hope that they may have that job: rather the reverse. They assume that some rival may achieve unexpected status instead.

One specific situation in which people fear loss of

status through change at work is where a manager thinks he will lose his personal secretary because of the introduction of word processing. This is a delicate point which needs to be handled with consummate tact, given that everyone thinks that their job is 'a little bit different' and that all their letters are 'one-offs'. The question is inevitably: Do they need to be one-offs? An interesting example is to be found at the Head Office of a large international company, where the Administrative Manager's secretary now handles far more complex and varied responsibilities than in the past, since virtually all her typed work is done by the word processing bureau.

Many secretaries themselves fear the installation of word processing, fearing that it will turn them into WP operators. These early fears have largely been dissipated by a general realisation that people who cannot change their attitudes may have to change their jobs. It is not long, either, before secretaries at all levels come to recognise that word processing enhances their jobs by reducing or removing those repetitive parts of it that they were never keen on anyway: long, confidential, technical reports, for example.

Loss of standing can also result if, as a consequence of change at work, some staff no longer have telephones on their desks. Some people will see this as tantamount to cutting off all their lines of communication. Many of us will remember the 'buzz' we felt when we got our first phone on our desks in our far-off days as office juniors. Now, to use a phone they may have to ask permission of a former rival, or use a call-box, or simply not use the phone at all as part of their work. At its worst, this can cause an acute feeling of social isolation and a fear that 'nobody will want to talk to me', and this feeling of alienation can act as a serious demotivator since some staff will feel that the company now considers them unfit to speak to other departments or to customers.

Fear of job loss

Not unnaturally, those who work in an office converting to computerised systems will have a very real fear of job loss. New people will be afraid that, on a 'last in, first out' basis, they will lose their jobs. Older staff may fear that their suspected inability to cope will force them to accept jobs of lower status, that is if they do not stand to lose their position in the company altogether.

In many organisations, unions and managements have concluded 'new technology agreements' which guarantee that there will be no redundancies as a result of the introduction of new technology. However, these agreements do not always cover reductions in staffing levels overall and, in those unfortunate cases where staff do not always trust the information given to them by management, the staff will not always believe management assurances that jobs will not be lost.

In such an atmosphere of distrust, fears of job loss tend to dominate and to cause intense anxiety. In some cases neither unions nor managements have been able to allay these fears. As a result, supervisors will have to cope with reduced productivity and motivation while staff devote the bulk of their energies to wondering whether they can depend on continuing employment. Later in this chapter there are guidelines for the supervisor faced with this problem of redundancy.

Health and safety

Although health and safety are dealt with in detail in Chapter 7, they must be mentioned briefly here. Staff are bound to express deep reservations about danger to eyesight and other supposed health hazards. Often, these will be the results of talking to someone who knows someone who started getting headaches just at the same time as their company computerised. This kind of third-hand, circumstantial trivia has virtually no foundation in fact, but it is important if only because people believe it to be true. Associated with these often groundless fears of VDUs is a degree of anxiety about the new working environment. Many organisations go to a great deal of trouble to redecorate, re-equip, install new lighting and so on, only to produce an atmosphere which many of your staff will condemn as 'over-sanitised' or 'just like a hospital'. These are often the very same people who, last month, were complaining about the lack of ventilation or the poor quality of the carpet. When they are faced with computerisation, the old office suddenly assumes qualities akin to Shangri-La.

Fear of 'exposure'

Many people – perhaps most of us – have a dark hidden area where we feel we have failed. An accounts clerk may be a terrible speller, or someone who handles customer complaints charmingly on the telephone may be totally innumerate. A surprising number of people are functionally illiterate and, being ashamed of this, will go to endless ingenious lengths to conceal the fact.

Major changes at work will cause much anxiety among people who fear that their shortcomings will be discovered, and that someone will find out, after all these years, that they still cannot work out percentages or whatever.

Because people are naturally ashamed of such weaknesses, they rarely discuss them with other people. If they did, they would discover that almost everyone has some bare patches where the educational system just didn't get through to them. Just the same, here is yet another layer of worry which the supervisor will have to penetrate when computerising an office.

Other personal fears

Besides these worries, which are fairly predictable, there may be other, less obvious areas of anxiety among staff in a changing office. These factors are things like losing desk drawers to house one's personal belongings, or being unable to see out of the window. People fear that they may lose all personality from their work areas. Their plants, posters, holiday postcards, comic slogans: all, they think, will be banished from the new office. The paraphernalia with which we commonly surround ourselves at work is part of the 'nesting' process which is extremely important in allowing each of us to retain some sort of identity. In an automated office, the need to 'nest' is even greater because of the increasing pressures towards conformity brought in by the new equipment.

There may also be worry over the loss of a neighbour, someone who has sat beside you for years and who is your regular companion at the pub on Fridays. Change may separate neighbours, or at least it may appear to threaten these relationships. Staff who have always worked with an unending flow of coffee or tea may not take kindly to the idea of having tea and coffee at times and in places dictated by someone else. One clerk who worked in a changing office had the habit of re-using her morning tea bag in the afternoon. Her major worry on the introduction of new furniture and equipment, was where she could keep the half-used tea bag between times. New regularised times for coffee and tea may make people feel that they are being treated like children, a feeling which frequently makes them behave in a very unhelpful manner.

Loss of promotion prospects

Because a newly-automated office may need a different type of staff, existing personnel are bound to worry that promotion prospects might be jeopardised by changes in the organisational structure. Perhaps, where school-leavers used to be adequate, graduates will need to form the bulk of future new recruits. Older staff who came as school-leavers themselves are sure to worry if they feel that a job towards which they have been working for years will either disappear altogether or, worse, be taken over by a young graduate who only joined the organisation six months earlier. When change is in the air, one of the commonest questions is 'Who's going to do my work?' If the answer is that the job will cease to exist in its present form, people will ask themselves if it ever was worth doing. They may, understandably, feel that they have wasted years doing it.

WHAT THE SUPERVISOR CAN DO TO HELP

It is not so much a question of what you can do to help in a changing office: it is essentially a matter of what you must do to get the results your boss wants and needs. You must understand and sympathise with people's fears, worries, niggles, qualms: whatever you call them, they will make life doubly difficult, particularly if, like so many people, your boss expects almost instant results from the new installation.

Understanding people's fears

You probably did not start your own working life as a supervisor. It is essential not only to make the effort to understand how your subordinates feel, but also to put yourself in their places and make sure that they know you understand and sympathise with their feelings.

You really will need to spell it out convincingly. It's no good saying 'I know how you feel' and then dashing off somewhere else, leaving people thinking you don't really mean a word of it. It's an important part of your job as supervisor to know your people well enough to be able to recognise the area which will present the greatest problems for each of them.

You may no longer be able to work flexitime, which may create difficulties for people who have to collect small children from school, or who have elderly relatives at home. Staff who do not drive may have problems with transport because of new work-hours which the system may demand. Shift work may become an issue, and you're bound to have some staff worrying about their social life as a result.

The supervisor's attitude to change

No office can become automated without a great upheaval and it is important to remember that your own attitude will have a strong bearing on the way your staff feel. If you project a positive approach to the whole exercise, you will find that it spreads to others and colours their attitudes as well. Enthusiasm is far more infectious than we sometimes recognise, and all supervisors should take care to show consciously and often their enthusiasm for change of whatever kind. In a word, if you are half-hearted about the new system, you cannot in all conscience expect your staff to co-operate enthusiastically. This point is dealt with in detail in Chapters 5 and 6.

Knowing where you are before you start

As supervisor, you need to know all there is to know about the work of your department. You need to know what is done, who does it and how often they do it. You need to know where your paperwork comes from and where it goes when your department has finished with it. You need to know the problem areas, the unpopular jobs and the easy options. You should be able to identify potential danger spots and, for all these points, you should have the answer to the question: 'Why?'.

Your own experience will probably help a great deal in analysing the work of your section. However, there is a limit to what you can learn from your own desk. Make time to get away from your own work area at intervals and Walk the Job. This means physically going round the department, doing some of the jobs your clerks do, answering the phone now and again, and getting first-hand experience of life in the front line. Use people's equipment to give yourself a totally objective view of how well it works. Try phoning the department from outside, to find out what your customers hear when they ring you up.

Like most supervisors who imagine that they are

thoroughly familiar with the department's work, you will probably get a few surprises.

Supervisors cannot steer the department through change without knowing where they are starting from. Equally, they must know what they are aiming at. These two points are simple enough, and everyone can grasp their significance when starting out on a holiday trip. Unfortunately, few of us are very good at relating these simple truths to our work.

EXPLAINING THE CHANGES

Change has to be handled systematically. You need a timetable with target dates for each stage of the change, and you must be absolutely clear in your own mind what the changes are going to be, and what their purpose is. It is most important for you to be able to explain clearly and convincingly the reasons for the upheaval. Computerisation for its own sake is not an adequate reason: you must be able to see further than the VDU screen. Computerisation can save time, money and energy. It can relieve people of boring jobs, and it can standardise and rationalise procedures and information throughout the organisation. It can leave time for better customer service: very few staff will disagree with these potential benefits.

In fact, this is where old-fashioned benefit selling comes in. Staff will respond much more readily to change if you can highlight the ways in which they will be better off. This is where it is so important for you to know the intimate details of the work done by your section or department. Only then can you pinpoint those elements of the work which staff have in the past disliked or found monotonous. They may not have bothered to tell you so, thinking that nothing will ever be done about it anyway. Your credibility will improve considerably when people realise that you always knew this or that job was boring, but that you could do little about it and that it will now be done by the computer.

Look out for bottlenecks which have irritated staff, and show them how these will be reduced or eliminated. As an example, think of one person having to check the work of others. After computerisation, this checking will need to be done less often, if at all, which will create a smoother workflow pattern. Some staff will respond enthusiastically to changes in job titles, and membership of a user group (see pp. 80–2) will enable people to feel that they are a genuine part of the changing office scene. You should take trouble to sell to staff the benefits which these changes will bring.

Another advantage which is well worth selling is the speed with which information will be available in future. This is where you can do some benefit selling on behalf of the customer or client, rather than directly for the staff. People who deal with customers direct will be delighted to know that they will be able to give faster, more up-to-date and more accurate information than in the past.

Don't oversell the change

It is easy to paint an idyllic picture of the trouble-free paperless office, and nothing could be further from the truth. Even if the manufacturer or supplier has oversold your boss on the advantages of change, try to keep your own wits about you and don't get carried away. If you don't keep your feet on the ground, you will have to cope with a great deal of disappointment, to say nothing of loss of face when the expected miracle fails to happen. Remember, too, that your clients may feel let down if you promise them too much too soon. These clients may not be actual paying customers or outside organisations. They are just as likely to be client departments or other sections of your organisation who are expecting to receive faster, neater and more accurate information than in the past.

You, the supervisor, have a vital 'link' role to play in making sure that your clients are happy with the service as it develops. Go and see them, to explain how the change is proceeding and what developments they can expect next. If you are too busy to make personal visits to your users, you should not be surprised if they complain about the low level of service they are getting. In any case, you need this 'customer feedback' to give you an objective view of your progress, and you will find the feedback invaluable if you pass it on to your staff so that they too know what effect their work has on others.

Timetabling change

All change takes time, and computerisation takes approximately twice as long as you first thought. Chapter 5 will deal in more detail with communication, but for the present consider a timetable as a means of communicating progress to your staff. Make it clear and detailed, taking into account all the factors you know about, and leaving some slack for the things you could never have predicted. 'Flu epidemics fall into this category, but staff holidays certainly do not. If you have some supervisory experience you will know the importance of building in a contingency factor, in other words, planning for crises. If you are new to supervision, this is the time to start systematically building into any plan enough leeway to enable you to retrieve the situation when it is obvious that it is not going according to plan.

Your timetable for change should include the dual running of the two systems, old and new. It is essential to retain the backup of the familiar old system while making sure the bugs are removed from the new way you are going to work. There is a potential problem here which you should try to anticipate. Inevitably your attention will be drawn to those people who are working the new system. This is an excellent way to split your department into 'haves' and 'have nots', so do make an effort to pay attention to those who may, for the moment, have a less glamorous role to play. This situation is particularly common in a typing pool which also has a few word processors. Visitors, anxious to see the new machines, make regular trips to see the VDUs, helping to give WP operators an exaggerated idea of their status and importance, which has been aptly described as that of 'the front row of the chorus'.

You need to include in your timetable the training provisions you are making. People should know that they will receive training, and they will also want to know what kind of training it will be, where it will take place, how long it will go on for, who will do it and whether they will be trained individually or in groups. They will want to know who will do their own work while they are training, so make sure you have an answer for this.

Don't forget to plan for double the quantity of stationery supplies you are used to, and remember, too, that VDUs are usually quite a bit bigger than conventional equipment: 50 per cent larger is a good rule of thumb. While equipment is being installed you may expect considerable dislocation of the normal office, if not controlled chaos. There will be trailing cables, cardboard cartons, extra installation personnel from the supplier. Not only will these

Word processors in a 'typing pool'. A supervisor is pointing out a sentence he would like changed; the operator can make the change at the touch of a key. Word processors are most people's first encounter with office automation; they are nowadays extremely popular with management and operators alike.

people need extra cups of coffee, they will also want to know where the toilets are, they may leave cigarettes in dangerous places and the noise level may prevent anyone from concentrating very effectively. If you are serving customers directly, you would be well advised to let them know that for the installation period things may not run quite as smoothly as usual. This is a ploy which will give you extra standing in your customers' estimation, since it usually has the effect of preventing quite as much chaos as you feared. It is, in a word, just another crisis contingency plan.

The timetabling of your changeover plan should not just be a set of ideas in your own mind. You, and everyone else, will be better able to cope with change if you chart the timetable diagrammatically, using graph paper for precision. Chapter 5 will provide ideas for using your department's creativity to help you to get the plan right.

The timetable should of course cover the period of dual running, and should allow for the running down of the previous system once you are satisfied that the computerised system is running without a hitch. One supervisor found himself faced with increasing demands for filing cabinets after computerisation was completed. On investigation, he discovered that he had forgotten to tell one of his filing clerks to stop keeping and filing some of the previously-used paperwork. The result was that, far from the paperless office, the paper was increasing faster than ever.

USER GROUPS

The data processing department will normally head a user group, which is an essential part of any office automation project. The members of the group will normally be the heads of departments or supervisors who will be affected by the change. If your organisation regards a user group as anything less than vital, you may expect problems which may continue to sour relations for months, if not years. Much has been written about the Yorkshire Metropolitan Borough, which in the late 'seventies rushed into word processing, making a number of staff redundant and precipitating a strike in the process. To quote two of their present supervisors, 'We are still living with the effects of that episode'. For the purposes of managing a smooth office change the group should meet weekly from the time the scope of the project is identified up to the time when it is no longer a novelty. Thereafter, meetings should be held monthly to ensure that liaison is maintained between all departments affected.

A user group meeting prevents the DP department from getting out of tune with the needs of the departments for which it is designing the system. It makes no difference whether the DP department is a part of the organisation, or consists of people hired to carry out a specific, finite, project. The brief is to design a workable system and, without regular contact with user departments, DP staff can easily run off the rails without intending to.

The benefit of a user group meeting for the user departments is that they get to know each other better, and understand more clearly what each is trying to do and how each departmental function relates to others. Most people in offices insist that they know all there is to know about what other departments do, and they are almost always wrong. The supervisor or manager will gain from hearing the views of others doing similar jobs to yours, and you can learn a great deal from such meetings, especially if you are a good listener: throwaway lines, assumptions, suggestions are all invaluable opportunities for learning from others.

REDUNDANCY

Redundancy is the problem which the supervisor will fear the most. As soon as change at work is mentioned, the possibility of redundancy will come into people's minds and it will grow, fester and poison relationships and atmospheres unless the supervisor takes it in hand and faces the problem squarely.

First, it is important to recognise that automation does not automatically mean redundancy. This is an important point to make to your staff if you are in the unenviable position where your own boss cannot yet reassure you that your section will not suffer job-losses. There is, in fact, increasing evidence to indicate that automation at work may have the reverse effect by creating new jobs where none existed before.

Some organisations undertake automation only on condition that they maintain their existing establish-ment levels. Typically, the workload increases, particularly in word processing. More uses are found for word processing, and the process of computer-isation takes far longer than anticipated. The creation of the automated database is often more complex than expected. As a result, and this is particularly the case in the public sector, the establishment level is supplemented by temporary workers on contract, sometimes in fairly large numbers over contract periods such as six months, often renewable.

Secondly, if redundancies are obviously on the horizon, you must pay as much attention to those you will lose as you do to those who will remain.

Important though it is to train your staff in the use of new equipment and techniques, it is also essential to retain the goodwill and commitment of staff who are leaving you. You never know when you may ask them to return on a temporary basis, even permanently perhaps. Also, the way you say 'goodbye' to redundant staff will colour not only their own attitude to the company, but that of their family and friends as well.

This is where another important point becomes relevant. If you do have to make staff redundant, try to train them before they leave in the systems you are introducing. This has a dual benefit: they can help you out in a crisis if you need them, and you will have the satisfaction of knowing that you are sending them out on to the job market with as much up-to-date training as you can manage. Some supervisors are under the false impression that attending courses will give them the magic password to painless redundancy. There is no such thing: you must face facts, and the key is to be as honest as you possibly can with people. Most people would far rather know where they stand than have a supervisor who waffles on for week after week trying to pretend that everyone will still have a job in a year's time.

You have a duty to do all you reasonably can for people whose jobs are to disappear during reorganisation. Help them as constructively as you can by allowing time for interviews, and giving them access to the phone to reply promptly to advertisements they read in the press. Whatever their age, nearly everyone can benefit from a few refresher techniques on how to apply for jobs, complete application forms, write letters: in a word, how to sell themselves. Try to highlight the person's best attributes and qualities so as to show them how they can 'sell' themselves to a prospective employer.

Encourage them to obtain relevant help and information from government agencies or from local resource groups.

MANAGING CHANGE AT WORK: A SUMMARY

It is the supervisor's job to anticipate people's worries, and to sympathise with and understand them. Change at work can be accomplished smoothly and efficiently with the cooperation of staff who know what is going to happen, when, and how they will be affected by it.

The supervisor's own enthusiastic approach will spread among the department and will help to ensure commitment to automation and subsequent success. Dual systems and user groups are essential, and it is vital, too, to take an honest, commonsense attitude to possible redundancy.

Case Study: International Charity

Voluntary organisations are particularly conscious of the need to keep administration costs to a minimum. As early as 1975, this organisation began to take the first steps towards a computerisation system which would enable them to keep a far closer check on their money, both incoming and outgoing. Income came from a variety of sources: local authority grant aid, legacies, covenants, gifts in kind, cash through a nationwide chain of branches, donations from commerce and industry, income from special social events, a company trading in a variety of gift items and so on.

The main objective was to create a system by which records of this money could be kept in a more systematic and accessible form. It was also hoped that it would require fewer staff to run the system, which in the past had consisted of a number of very repetitive jobs.

Outgoing funds were mostly payments for the rental of project premises, medical and other supplies and weekly cheques for hourly-paid staff on outside projects. There were also payments for stationery, utilities, printing etc. Monthly-paid staff were paid via an outside bureau.

The department which was mainly concerned with computerisation was the Donations Department which consisted of a departmental head, his deputy and 11 clerical/secretarial staff. The plan was to reduce staff by approximately half. This could have been a difficult situation but for two factors. Firstly, there was no union presence which might have caused opposition and secondly, about half the existing staff were already at or over retiring age.

Staff were told about the impending computerisation at an early stage. Those whose jobs would disappear were, in the main, those who were over retirement age and the job of informing these staff fell to the deputy head of the department, because he had a particularly sympathetic and understanding approach, and enjoyed the trust of his section of the department.

Because the size of the organisation did not allow for the employment of full-time systems and programming staff, short-term personnel were hired. Because they were strangers to the organisation and did not share the corporate value system, they were not universally welcomed and were, in fact, viewed with considerable suspicion.

A User Group was set up, and held monthly meetings. The purpose of the group was to keep departmental heads and their deputies in touch with the analysts and programmers, and with the general progress of the project. The managers and deputies were in turn responsible for passing on to their departments news of the latest stages of progress.

As time went on, it became clear that the clerical staff were finding it more and more difficult to understand the new system. The main cause of this was that some of the departmental managers had difficulty in understanding and communicating the finer points of the system.

The secretarial and clerical staff spent much time discussing their worries and fears, particularly over such matters as the design of input forms, and the space allocated on such forms for the names of donors. Consequently, they felt left out of the mainstream of the project and became very cynical over the original time scale. This was rapidly approaching fruition, with no obvious signs that the project was in fact near completion.

An emergency occasion arose when some of the clerical staff had to deputise for the deputy head of the department, and this was a turning point in the involvement of the staff at the lower levels. They found that they could make significant contributions to the discussions, highlighting points which their seniors had overlooked. Their self-confidence and enthusiasm grew as a result, and they very soon began making constructive suggestions, some of which were adopted.

The project did not reach completion on schedule, but a Computer Users Group was established which consisted of those who were inputting data, actually at the 'coal face' so to speak. Some of the more senior managers had had reservations about the system, and had found it difficult to grasp some of the concepts. More junior staff, often with lower education levels, caught on more quickly, and some older staff, in subordinate jobs, found themselves keenly interested in the computerisation in spite of themselves.

Interdepartmental relationships improved as computerisation spread through the organisation, and people met more of their colleagues. They came to understand more clearly the actual, as opposed to the imagined, functions of the rest of the organisation.

The system is now, by and large, taken for granted. There

are still some doubters and not everyone is totally behind the system. It is fair to say that without the Computer Users Group, consisting of more junior staff, implementation would have been far more difficult. A word processor is now in use, and is operated by a young man who had been a redundant typesetter. He makes very full use of its information handling facilities, as well as the normal text processing features and is extremely enthusiastic about office technology: possibly marginally more so than the bulk of his colleagues.

5 Communication and consultation

Consulting and communicating with staff are the twin means by which the successful supervisor involves staff and gains their commitment to almost every aspect of daily work. This chapter explains the methods and the advantages of systematic channels of communication and consultation in any organisation.

First a definition of communication, which is 'creating understanding in the minds of other people'. By 'understanding', one does not necessarily mean simply an understanding of the words used. That, of course, is essential, but more than that it implies a sympathy with the implications of those words and the way in which they are used. Following on from this, communication suggests – even demands – a commitment to and agreement with the message being conveyed.

Effective communication is an outstanding way to establish the leadership role in the working group. This done, the challenge is to maintain the position. Supervisors may achieve respect when first appointed, and may later fail to retain the regard of their subordinates. Nobody has to respect anybody: the days are long past when position automatically guaranteed respect. Most supervisors will agree that respect has to be earned, and that you need continuously to do those things which earned you that respect in the first place. In other words, you cannot expect it to last without regular polishing.

COMMUNICATION BETWEEN PEOPLE

When two people attempt to communicate with each other, they are faced with several layers of insulation which tend to prevent effective communication taking place. Most of the time we use oral or written media, usually supported by gestures, and although we genuinely try we frequently fail to 'get through' to people, without necessarily even being aware of our failure.

It is the responsibility of the communicator to put the message across and it is pointless to blame someone for not understanding you if you use jargon unfamiliar to your listener. In particular, of course, you need to be thoroughly familiar with the language of computing, so that you can teach it to your staff and enable them to understand exactly what it all means. You can rarely communicate effectively if you are not sure about the subject yourself. The glossary at the end of this book should help in creating the necessary level of understanding.

When computerisation is first mentioned, many people may give the impression that they understand all about it. This may in many cases be true, but you should take account of people who are nervous of admitting that some phrases actually mean nothing to them: they are repeating, parrot-fashion, something they have heard from someone else. Their nervousness may stem from shyness, in junior staff, or senior staff may be afraid of exposing their lack of understanding. Either way, it is the duty

A personal secretary and her word processor. Together, she and her boss are designing a document on the word processor's screen. This kind of task becomes quick, easy and satisfying with the help of a word processor.

of the supervisor to check individual understanding on this, as on any other point regarding change at work. The quality of the questions you use to establish the appropriate level of comprehension will directly affect the quality of the answers. Questions beginning with why, when, where, what and who will produce far better replies than those which allow a yes or no response.

Some people may genuinely believe that they understand the jargon, and may assume that others do so as well. Take the word 'word' for example. It is commonly associated with 'word processing', which gives the impression that a word processor is simply a computer which processes words instead of numbers, and so it does. However, in computer terminology a *word* is a unit of storage in a computer:

8 bits = 1 byte
2 or more bytes = 1 word, depending on the
        size of the computer

Originally word processors were known as 'text processors', which is in fact what they are, as distinct from data processors – computers which are designed to process text rather than information. However, the widespread adoption of the term 'word processing' has led some people seriously to underestimate the capabilities of word processors, treating them as if they were merely high-powered typewriters.

Besides jargon and assumptions, people's resentments and fears of change prevent them from fully understanding what is being said or written to them. This is particularly the case with senior secretaries who may fear that they will become downgraded to clerks or WP operators. Many managers, too, resent any suggestion that automation could possibly improve office systems which they consider to be already perfect. People with these sharp-edged attitudes need to be calmed by being given a clear timetable of the changes planned, as well as extra reassurance that the only parts of their job to disappear will probably be the parts they least liked in the first place. They also need to be kept in touch with the pace of the change. Their fears are usually caused by emotive visions of their offices being transformed overnight into 'cells' devoid of both soul and paper. Many people, asked about the 'paperless office', would give a hollow laugh and point to the enormous quantities of computer print-outs which threaten to spill over into every corner of the office.

COMMUNICATING WITH YOUR STAFF

It is essential for you to be able to keep your staff in touch with whatever is going on in the company. A clerk in an insurance company was asked who his boss was. He pointed to the shop steward, who was not, in fact, his supervisor. The shop steward had been accorded the status of 'boss' because in the clerk's mind she was the one who passed on company information. It is easy to see how a supervisor can lose ground in a situation like this. It is also easy to understand how dangerous it is for staff relationships.

A great many companies make no attempt to communicate to people at the lower end of the hierarchy. At the lower levels, people often do not know what the company makes, who is the managing director and so on. Yet the managing director may be heard bewailing the fact that staff cannot identify with those at board level, and vice versa. This should hardly come as a surprise if board members work behind closed doors in faceless anonymity. In Chapter 6 there are many examples and suggestions for increasing motivation. The majority of them are simple matters of communication from the top of the organisation down, and from the bottom up.

Some organisations consider communication so important that they take time out to run regular communication meetings. What these meetings are called really does not matter. What does matter is that they are held regularly, briefing people face to face in their normal working teams, giving them relevant information somewhere where they feel relaxed and receptive.

Regular meetings

Many people, if their boss calls them into the office, start wondering what they have done wrong or, worse, fearing that they are to be made redundant. With this in mind they build up a mental armour of worry and resentment which most bosses find it difficult, if not impossible, to penetrate. Most often, the summons leads to bad news. It should not surprise the supervisor, therefore, if your team automatically associate such meetings with negative events. In fact many managers, asked how often they pass on information to their staff, explain that they speak to them when they need telling off or when a factory is closing down. This can hardly help relationships at work between those who lead and those who follow. Remember that once you are a supervisor you are part of management, one of 'them', and you need to do all you can to minimise the gap which can appear between different levels of staff.

If you fail to hold regular meetings with your staff,

you place yourself and the department at the mercy of the grapevine. Of all the plants people try to grow in offices, the grapevine flourishes the best. It can cause untold harm to relationships, and in no area more than in office automation. Rumours of the numbers of staff to be made redundant, the departments which will cease to exist, the processes in paperflow which are to be carried out at another branch of the company: all these and many more are typical of the kind of stories which people believe. The fact that they are untrue is immaterial: if people believe them, that is enough to do the damage.

Grapevines, however, have one positive aspect, which is that they do at least indicate that people are sufficiently interested in the organisation to gossip about what goes on. As a wise supervisor, you should seize this particular benefit and use it to your advantage. Use your regular meetings to scotch rumours and to give the correct version of the story.

Rumours almost always have a germ of truth in them. However, because they become distorted and are almost always negative, management becomes the villain of the piece, and the reasons for taking certain decisions become twisted out of all recognition. Your staff need someone they can rely on for the correct version of whatever rumour is current at the time. If you establish a pattern of regular meetings, part of whose purpose is to give the full story, you will find that you have built up a mutual trust which will be the envy of your colleagues.

Communicating face to face

Many organisations, especially very large ones, consider that communication with the work force is effectively done through notice boards or printed notices sent to everyone. When primitive methods like this fail, they express pained surprise.

Written communication can mean one thing to one person, and something totally different to another. It can be misunderstood unless oral explanation is added.

Similarly, although oral communication allows for questions if people do not understand, there is a need for a written backup in case key points are forgotten.

Communicating face to face is a way of 'selling' the organisation's message and viewpont. That is why it is no part of the union's job to pass on management's information in a convincing manner.

Supervisors can sometimes be heard telling their staff what is going on, prefacing their remarks with such phrases as 'What I gather is . . .', or 'Apparently . . .', or worst of all 'It says here . . .'. These introductions to the management message take most of the value out of the statement. Your job as supervisor includes 'selling' the management message as if it were your own. It will not always be easy and there are bound to be occasions when you will hate having to do it. Consider the consequences of failure to 'sell' effectively: if you display any shadow of disloyalty to your own boss by using the phrases above, you can hardly be surprised if your subordinates show a corresponding disloyalty to you.

When you pass on information face to face, not only can you do a better 'selling' job, but you can also introduce a strong element of enthusiasm, which is a vital weapon in your armoury when you are managing change. Your own enthusiasm, effectively communicated, can carry the whole team along with you with a minimum of disruption. This will never be an easy job, though. Supervisors are often asked for help and advice on which type of computer they consider might be best suited to the work their department does. There are numerous cases on record of managements subsequently buying the complete opposite of the supervisor's suggestion. Picture yourself, then, having to explain to your own staff the decision which management has made. There is no point in emphasising the fact that your advice has been ignored, unless you really want to highlight to your juniors the fact that your superiors have overruled you without explanation. It is much better to find out the reasons for the choice, emphasise them, look on the bright side and try to sell such advantages as you can identify. No decision, management or otherwise, is ever perfect and we often have to content ourselves with the 'least worst' way out. Point this out to your staff and be thankful that someone has at least made a decision. Indecisive managements are seldom popular, to put it mildly.

Communicating with everyone together

Grapevines often have their firmest roots in quick informative chats given by a supervisor who has a word, first with this one, then with the other, then with a third and so on. This is a very time-consuming system, as well as being extremely harmful. If you communicate orally to several people at different times it is virtually impossible to give exactly the same message, omitting nothing and giving exactly the same emphasis and inflection to each word and phrase. Consequently, everyone will put different interpretations on what has been said to them. In addition, it is human nature, once one has been told something by one's boss, to want to share it with a colleague. Then the grapevine really takes a hold as two, three or more versions become mixed up and misinterpreted. Far better, then, to give out information to the team as a group together. Apart from keeping your information accurate and undiluted, you save a great deal of time and energy.

A further danger of communicating 'piecemeal' is that it can give rise to impressions that you have 'favourites', and there are few better ways to splinter the team spirit you have so carefully built up. If people are absent on account of sickness or holiday, make a careful note to brief them as soon as they return.

You may wonder how to handle team communication if you have people working in shifts. Some organisations, for example, have a twilight word processing shift from 6 pm to 10 pm. In this instance, arrange an overlap of, say, fifteen minutes, but it is important to brief people in company time. You cannot expect shift workers to sacrifice an hour's pay because you have not yet taken control of your time.

Giving relevant information

Most employees consider themselves poorly informed about what goes on in their organisations. On the other hand, if they are handed the company's Annual Report and Accounts they will very quickly switch off, totally bemused by the figures. The type of information people want is, for example, how many invoices they cleared last week, or who earned a bonus for exceeding the standard key depressions per hour. This is local information, on items which affect people in their day-to-day work. You will not find that the organisation's exact cash flow situation will excite very much interest; the proposed extension of the sports club facilities certainly will, and so will the redecoration of the canteen.

Staff like to know when the company is starting a new advertising campaign. One Fleet Street daily paper makes sure all its staff know when its advertisements are due to appear on television, and a major oil company does the same. This information encourages greater commitment to the organisation, its products and its objectives.

When an office is going through a process of computerisation it is essential to keep people in touch. Many supervisors consider that they only need to tell people what is going on when things are going wrong. Of course, this is another way of associating management information with bad news, but, worse, it leaves people in the dark. A vehicle importing company decided to computerise its invoicing system, using one of its branches as a pilot project. Months passed and everything went according to schedule, but because central management gave out no new information staff in the branch concerned began to worry that the project was behind time, or had been abandoned. They felt sure that the rest of the company had been told what was happening and morale fell badly. Eventually, an outsider mentioned to the managing director this strong undercurrent of worry. The managing director was horrified and explained that everything was going exactly according to plan, adding a promise to let them know if things went off schedule. People need reassurance that everything is going well, not news that things are falling behind schedule. It is no coincidence that first-aiders are taught to reassure accident victims first of all, even if they can do no more than call an ambulance.

Holding your meeting in familiar surroundings

One of the aims of your briefing session is to break

down potential barriers between members of the team, and between management and subordinates. One of the worst places you can do this is in the boardroom, where people feel stiff and formal. Much better to hold an informal meeting in the normal work area. Then, if the phone rings, someone can take care of it. Many supervisors give the phone as an excuse for not holding meetings to brief their staff. If you actually count the number of times the phone rings during a half-hour period, it will probably be far less than you thought. In any event, if someone is stationed near the phone they can answer it, take messages, and catch up with the meeting when they return to the group.

A further advantage of briefing people on their home ground is that the communication meeting itself, by implication, forms an essential, normal part of the working day. Some organisations require staff to attend these meetings as a part of the job: other activities are planned around it, and dates are fixed a year in advance. Only emergencies are permissible excuses for non-attendance.

Subjects to be covered

Progress

Having gathered your team together, you may well wonder what you are going to talk to them about. First, and most important, is the answer to the collective question 'How are we doing?', that most basic of human questions. It forms, in a way, a group appraisal. Make sure you have plenty of relevant information on how the team have measured up since last they met. This part of the meeting may well consist of charts and figures and these will have far greater impact if they are visually appealing and, perhaps, shown on an overhead projector. Give each member of the team a photocopy which will help them to understand and relate to what you are telling them.

This is communication at its most sophisticated:

- information which relates directly to people's work
- visual images of what they have achieved, backed up by hard copy
- oral descriptions of team achievement
- everyone receiving the same information at the same time, the most effective grape-vine-herbicide ever invented
- encouragement and motivation from a team leader who uses this communication as an aid to greater commitment.

The type of progress will naturally vary according to the type of business carried on by the organisation, but here are a few examples:

- reduction of errors on invoices
- reduction of time spent doing a regular job on the word processor (eg company telephone list, organisation chart, Annual Report and Accounts)
- praise passed down from director level to the team through the supervisor
- increased sales figures
- fewer rejected input forms
- faster solution of problems.

Although the bulk of your progress information should be local, say about 70 per cent, save time for items of company progress. Be sure to tell your team about new products or new customers, large accounts won or contracts signed.

Information about people

Of course it will be important for staff to know who the managing director's replacement is to be, but local information has far more impact. Many people may have had the experience of joining a department only to find that not only were all the equipment, terminals etc. strange to you, but nobody in the department knew who you were or why you were there. Keep people in touch with comings and goings: people on Youth Training Schemes for instance, or visitors to the organisation who should be welcomed. Be sure to remind people about job vacancies they may have forgotten about, mention members of the team who have been selected to go on advanced function courses at the manufacturers or suppliers, and reassure people that there are no planned redundancies. Make sure that exchange visitors from other departments are welcome. The same goes for 'temps', but, above all, be sure that everyone is expecting new staff.

When you supervise a group of people whose jobs have a high boredom potential, it is more important than ever to highlight achievements which may not be directly related to work: winner of the darts cup, passing a driving test, leading role in the company pantomime. If a former operator is calling in just to say hello again, make sure everyone knows. Remind people of staffing problems which may arise during peak holiday periods. Tell staff what plans you have to cope with contingencies and give them plenty of time to organise themselves in case you have to ask them to do overtime. Pass on news from former colleagues who may now work for different departments. One oil company with several word processing centres organises a monthly newsletter which not only gives news of staff, but also provides a medium for people to contribute articles, recipes, jokes, DIY tips, cartoons and so on. The effect is to keep people together, thinking of the team they work in, and emphasising the role they have to play in making that team – your team – work well.

Matters of policy

If you are under the impression that your staff have at their fingertips all the items in the staff handbook, you would be wrong. There are often rules which go by the board and this section of your briefing meeting is for reminding people of points where you have noticed slackness. There are countless areas where people need a little nudging, for example:

- disc handling care
- cleaning screens daily for better vision
- office tidiness
- punctuality when working shifts, or at any other time.

There are other items which you can include here. The organisation may have a new policy on training people for promotion: this is your opportunity to tell people. The entire organisation may be closing for the Christmas/New Year week: tell people well in advance, so that they can plan their social life. If there are changes in the organisation's pension plan, let people know so that they can tell their families. Remind the team of the organisation's suggestion scheme. If canteen arrangements are to be changed, mention this so you can help to avoid chaos. Future plans for the organisation could come in here, such as new branches, expansion of manufacturing facilities, new overtime arrangements.

Lastly, on policy matters, do not for one moment think that once you have told people something they will remember it. Their memories are short, and just as a garden needs regular doses of fertiliser so your team needs reminders and booster shots of enthusiasm from you.

Points for action

It is always therapeutic to end a meeting with practical ideas of things people need to do. Here you could include the importance of deciding on holiday dates, to prevent a rush of absences during the peak holiday period. Set a target date for holidays to be notified, and stick to it. Emphasise the need for the department to continue to provide its service throughout the year, whether operators are on holiday or not.

In a changing office environment, with computers which are expected to jeopardise and alter ways of working, it is important to try and use this last part of your briefing to send people back to work with a buzz and a lift. Your own enthusiasm for changing technologies will go a long way to encouraging others to welcome rather than reject change. Enthusiasm is highly contagious, and you should make full use of it. Many people will try to avoid changing technology, putting off the evil day. They may feel that computers will swamp them and take them over. It is part of your job to emphasise the fact that people will only be swamped if they allow themselves to be: computers are totally useless without people to program and operate them and you must get this point across to the prophets of doom.

Organising your briefing

You may feel that you need to go on a public

speaking course before you can hold a briefing meeting successfully. Nothing could be wider of the mark. You do, of course, need to prepare yourself, with notes, figures, charts and so on: never try to brief a group without preparation. Make sure you know exactly what you are going to say, even to the point of learning your first sentence off by heart: this will relax you and give you the confidence to continue. If you think your hands will shake, put your notes on your desk or table top. Only write notes on one side of the card or paper, and use colour and headings to trigger off the important points. Make sure you are thoroughly familiar with your material; you will probably remember far more than you think. Never read notes from a card, unless you want to quote something verbatim. You may, for example, have had a charming memo from your boss, thanking you for coping so smoothly with the changeover from one computer to another: read it out, pin it up on a notice board and make sure everyone sees it.

However nervous you are, keep your hands out of your pockets: if you need to, put your hands behind your back. Try to avoid nervous mannerisms, like pulling at your ear or taking your glasses off and on: people will start to count the number of times you do each irritating thing, rather than listening to what you are saying. Use normal, everyday words, and abbreviations which everyone understands, but check that new staff really do understand. Use eye-contact to communicate, and to see that people have not switched off. Try to develop your own individual style, and make sure you keep to time. If you ramble on, people will become bored and might suggest that the meeting is a waste of time: much better to finish with people asking for more. When you have finished, say so, and encourage questions, first making sure that you have anticipated the questions and have the answers ready.

Your regular meetings should eventually become part of the woodwork, so to speak, with the accolade of their own nickname: family prayers or something similar. If this happens, you can feel well satisfied that you have a success on your hands.

Other ways to communicate

Appraisals

Many companies take a great deal of trouble to communicate with staff by means which are not always recognised as such. Take appraisal, for example. This is usually an annual event when the organisation tells you formally how it feels about your performance in the job, how you have coped with computerisation and the amount of new work you have had to learn. On another level, the organisation is appreciating the efforts you have made, and signalling that it is offering opportunities for further development in such areas as pro- gramming, supervising larger departments, holding familiarisation sessions for senior management.

Accountability charts

Your section ought to have an accountability chart which tells everyone what everyone else does and who they report to. These charts have to be updated frequently, and this is often given as an excuse for not having one. Word processors can cope with this type of revision work without any trouble, so the chart can easily be updated, keeping information up to date. You should also have a chart or diagram which explains where your section fits in with other

sections and departments, or with parallel
departments in other locations of the organisation.
Not only is this a means of communication, it is also
a way in which office technology in the form of word
processors can keep information updated, accurate
and freely available, yet another aid to motivation
since people can see more easily where they fit in the
overall picture.

Company magazines

Most large organisations run an in-house publication
of some sort: magazine or weekly paper. These
publications are usually carefully written to give
maximum news and entertainment to staff, as well as
passing on company information. Make sure your
staff read it. Encourage shy juniors to contribute a
recipe, riddle, photograph or drawing. When you
know your people well enough, you will be able to
pick out the operator with 'A'-level art who could
design and produce a monthly strip cartoon
explaining the way your computerised department
works. This provides motivation for the junior, and a
better magazine as well.

Notice boards

Notice boards are notorious for being untidy and
consequently unread. Cynics will say that the only
way to get items read is to pin them upside down.
Others, less hardened, put a 'take down' date at the
bottom of each notice. This will only work, though,
if you act on the system: if you say 25 May, stick to
25 May. You will find that this sparks people's
attention to the notices.

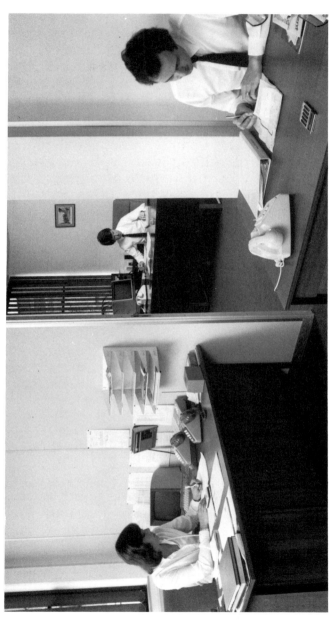

A modern office; both the secretary and her manager have computer terminals on their desks. She can type documents in draft and let him check them on his screen before they are printed. They also share a diary with everyone else in their department; the screen shows everyone's appointments within one display, making it much quicker to set up meetings.

COMMUNICATING UPWARDS

Suggestion schemes

Many organisations have profited greatly from
listening to the ideas of their junior staff. If your
organisation has a suggestion box, encourage people
to use it by pointing out the benefits available to you
if your idea is adopted. Usually these take the form
of financial rewards. Often ideas will be totally
impracticable, but it is important to give them a try.
If you never try out other people's ideas you will
stifle this important creativity at the bottom level,
simply because people will be too demoralised to
bother to think things up. Their attitude will, understandably, be that you are paid to think up new
ideas, not them, and they will not easily see why
they should help you.

Consultation

Consultation is not, as many people think, asking
your subordinates how you should run the business
because you cannot think how to do so unaided.
Consultation is asking people for ideas which will
help you to make better decisions, and it is a way of
letting people feel that they are contributing directly
to their working conditions.

In decision-taking, consultation becomes crucial.
Having established that the decision is yours to take,
your next step should be to consult your staff. You
are asking them for their opinions on the subject and
for suggestions, ideas and help which will enable
you to make a decision secure in the knowledge that
you have the commitment of the people who will
have to help you implement it. When, through
consultation, people feel that they have had a part to

play in the way a new system is installed, they are far more likely to work hard to make it work well.

As an example, consider the situation of having to move furniture to accommodate an extra member of staff. The decision that you have already taken is that this new member of staff is necessary, and that you need to move furniture to fit in the necessary work station. You may have drawn up a floor plan, ordered the furniture, seen to the rewiring and cabling, and arranged for specialist help in moving terminals, processing units and heavy furniture.

Consultation should involve putting your plan to your department, explaining to them what you have done so far and why, and giving them time to consider your plan, with a deadline to make comments to you about it. You may, without realising it, have placed two deadly rivals side by side. You might have placed someone at the opposite end of the department from the stationery they need to use daily. You may have situated a printer with a high acoustic hood too near to a window to allow anyone to open the window in hot weather. If the window is opened, the breeze might cause havoc with the paper feed.

When people have had a chance to have their say, they will feel much more involved in the decision and the change will be accepted much more readily: after all, they were part of the decision-taking process. A further advantage of consultation is that, by setting up a controlled brainstorming session, you can encourage more and better ideas, which will enable you to take better decisions.

Having considered the opinions of those who work with you, and taken the decision, be sure to communicate the decision to all those whose depart-ments are affected by it. If you try to set up a unilateral system which in no way fits in with existing systems, you are heading for trouble. Nowhere is this more important than in a computerised office, where each system tends to hang carefully upon another, and where departmental co-operation assumes an importance it never had before.

COMMUNICATION AND CONSULTATION: A SUMMARY

Your staff need to know how they are doing and where they and the department fit into the corporate structure, and you need to make certain that the channels of communication, both upwards and downwards, remain open and freely used. Staff who are consulted about matters affecting them and the way they work will throw their weight behind you far more energetically, helping you, the team and the organisation.

Case Study: Legal Practice

Solicitors are not usually known for their forward-looking approach to office systems. Their prevailing value system is more often seen to suggest that professionalism and client-confidence result more from time-honoured routines than from microelectronic technology.

Surprisingly, therefore, many legal firms have been front-runners in the adoption of word processing, particularly since the accuracy of work is so important. Hardly less vital, given the boring and repetitive nature of much legal typing, is the need for a particular style of professional presentation on heavy paper which has often conspired to defeat the most conscientious typist.

This firm has, in less than two years, made a smooth and highly successful transition from stand-alone word processors to a shared-logic word processing system. The partnership initially made the decision that in no way would word processing be imposed on those who were uncertain and hesitant about their ability to learn to use it, or to benefit from it. At the time, there was a great deal of heavy supplier-advertising, which implied that there would be massive secretarial job-losses as a result of word processing.

Meanwhile, the Word Processing Manager was from the start totally involved in equipment evaluation, and asked for help in taking the decision as to the exact equipment needed for the work involved. Specifications were drawn up, and a short-list produced. At this stage, the Word Processing Manager and the Personnel Manager responsible for the secretarial staff were sent by the firm on a trip to the USA to evaluate the equipment on the short-list, and to suggest the most suitable for purchase.

The decision had been taken prior to this equipment changeover to use the word processors first in the high-profile, high-pressure department which dealt with court cases. The experiment was a great success, and the department was most enthusiastic about the improved work turnround. Consequently, word processing was gradually introduced into other departments, and further equipment ordered. This had been the intention in the first place, but the partner in charge of the installation was anxious that departments should request word processing rather than having it suggested to them, or worse, thrust upon them.

It would be a mistake to suggest that the installation took place, and was later expanded, without a strong case being made to the partnership generally. A great deal of money was involved in the investment, and it was by no means a *fait accompli*. It was, however, successful because of the careful approach and the appeal to staff by implicitly involving them in the decision. Legal practices make much use of standard text and paragraphs which appear as a matter of routine in some types of legal work — conveyancing and wills, for example. The potential for word processors to store and use these standard documents, therefore, was an essential facility in the changeover.

Although the DP department would have preferred to keep control of this aspect of the work, the decision was taken to retain the separation of DP from WP. By this means, the introduction of word processing did not bring with it further departmental upheavals and changes in accountability. The progression of the word processing has now extended to virtually all secretaries in the firm. None of them has proved unsuitable, and the training programme has overcome the bulk of the difficulties. This consists of two weeks' intensive training, during which time operators and secretaries learn only the functions which their work will demand. This is done in-house, and all training work is directly related to their future workloads. During the training period, no 'normal' work is done, and if they need it, operators and secretaries may have further 'brush-up' training sessions.

The Word Processing Manager does no operating as a normal part of the job, but is accountable for the productivity and accuracy of the word processing centres. Inter-departmental liaison is maintained by an in-house news sheet which keeps people in touch with each other, encourages the sharing of good ideas and 'tricks of the trade', as well as creating a valuable fellowship within and between all system users.

Far from appearing to work in the quill pen era, this firm of solicitors is making maximum use of word processing technology, with full commitment, enthusiasm and motivation from staff at all levels.

6 Gaining people's commitment

One of the most important characteristics which good leaders share is the knack of getting people's commitment to the job. Motivation is not just enthusiasm, and very rarely money: it is getting people to want to do, willingly and well, those things which you need them to do.

New supervisors often say that the first and often the only guidance their managers gave them was to 'Go out there and motivate them', without explaining how this feat was to be accomplished. This chapter identifies some of the many things you can do to get genuine commitment from your staff in such a way as to help you to get the job done better, faster and with fewer of the petty irritations you so often find in offices, especially during a period of change.

A great many supervisors feel that they have trodden this path before, and that their own bosses are the ones who need training in motivation. There are two answers to this problem. Firstly, you can manage upwards, setting an example by doing to your staff the things you wish your own boss would do to you; secondly, you can motivate your own boss in a variety of ways, none of which are difficult, and hardly any of which depend on an organisational structure which may in other ways hamstring you.

SOME MOTIVATIONAL THEORISTS

Most supervisors have at one time or another paid homage to the three American theorists Maslow, McGregor and Herzberg, or McHerzlow as they are sometimes called.

Maslow's steps (see Figure 6.1) are based on an ascending hierarchy of individual personal needs, starting with such basics as sleep and food, and rising through friendship to the need for a sense of personal accomplishment. McGregor (Figure 6.2) identified similar needs but formulated them into a pyramid, with basics at the bottom and self-fulfilment at the apex, suggesting the motivation can come from within rather than always from an external stimulus. This is the foundation of McGregor's X–Y Theory, which sets out certain assumptions that managers often make about their staff. Theory X people are something of a hybrid between Wackford Squeers in *Nicholas Nickleby* and Mr Gradgrind in *Hard Times.* In others words, they assume that people hate work, must be bribed to do it and show their greatest creativity when they are leadswinging their way round management rules.

On the opposite side of the coin, Theory Y people expect staff to enjoy their work, to seek responsibility and to impose on themselves a self-discipline far stricter than any their boss might demand. Most of us are a composite of both theories, with varying balances between X and Y. The importance of these distinctions is that people who are predominantly Theory X will treat their staff accordingly, and the result will be the familiar 'if you treat people like children, they'll behave like them'. If staff are assumed to be of subnormal intelli-

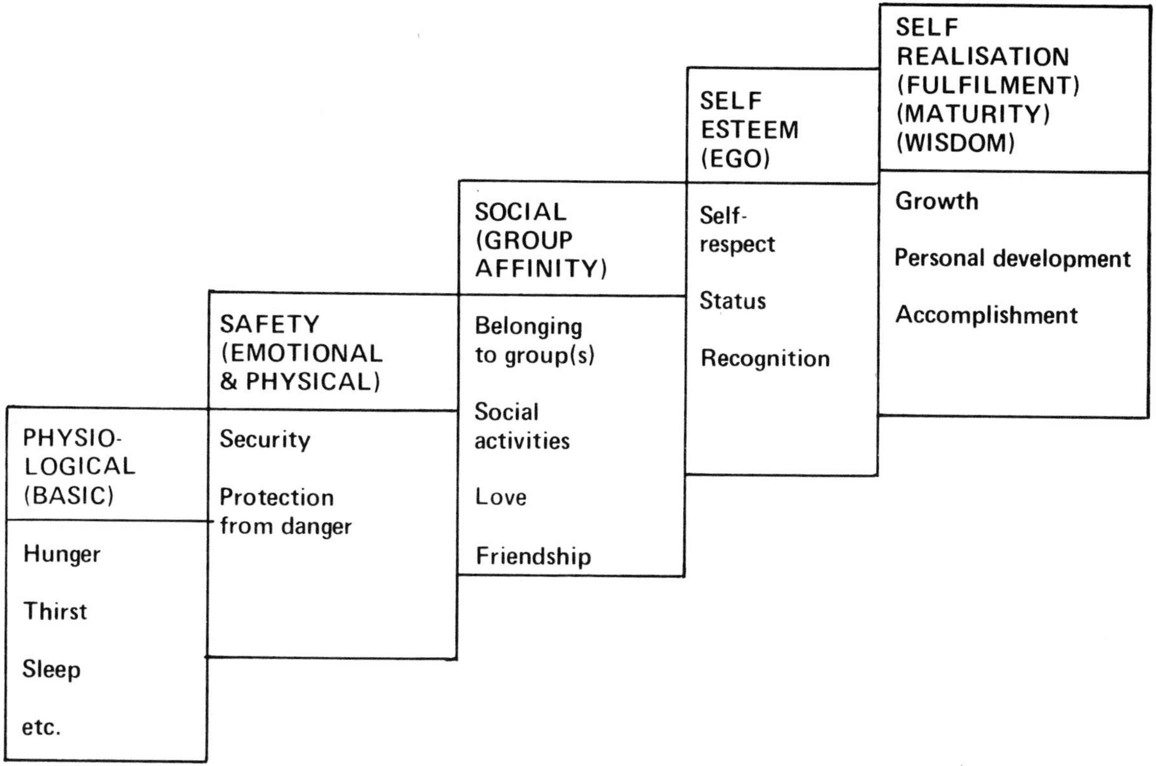

Figure 6.1 A hierarchy of personal needs (After A. H. Maslow, *Personality and Motivation*)

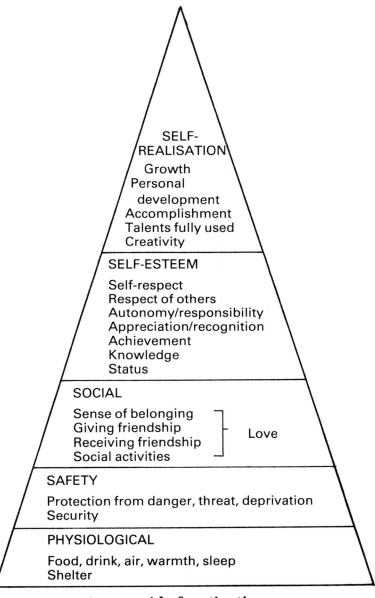

Figure 6.2   A pyramid of motivation
(After Douglas McGregor)

gence they will act out that assumption, and their self-respect will deflate like a tyre with a slow puncture, because at some point they are bound to ask themselves if perhaps their boss may not be right in treating them as morons.

At the other end of the scale, if people are given challenges and targets to meet, they will at least try to justify some of the faith you have implicitly shown in them. Most often, they succeed beyond their own wildest expectations.

A third theorist, Frederick Herzberg, produced a list of factors which made people either satisfied or dissatisfied with their work (Figure 6.3). Those which produced greatest satisfaction were intangibles, quite unrelated to money or working conditions. They included personal achievement, responsibility and recognition for a job well done. His findings show that the more these satisfying elements were included in people's work, the greater was their motivation to do that work.

On the other hand some factors, such as company policy and relationships with colleagues and superiors, had a strongly negative effect on people. Of greatest importance here is the fact that no matter how much you improve, say, working conditions or salary, you will not obtain a corresponding increase in people's commitment to their job if the sense of achievement, recognition and responsibility are absent. As an example, consider whether if someone doubled your salary you would produce twice the work.

Theories are useful, therefore, only if they help supervisors to understand their own staff and see what makes them 'tick'. What these theories do not do is give you any kind of action plan, things you can do to generate the enthusiastic activity and sense of purpose which you so badly need from your team. In

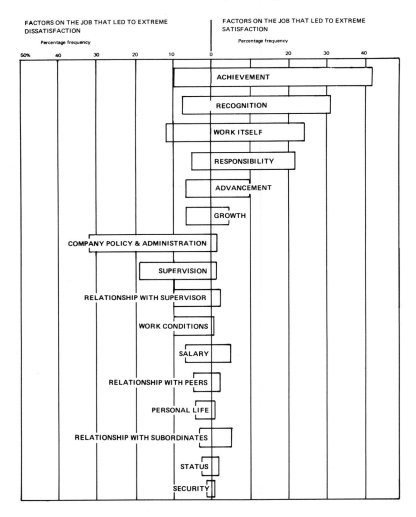

Figure 6.3   Positive and negative elements of work
(Reproduced by permission of Granada Publishing
Ltd from Frederick Herzberg's book *Work and the
nature of man*)

a changing office, where output may fall rather than rise during certain periods, user departments will complain loud and long and for this reason motivation is crucially important. A service department is just the type of department which is never noticed, never thanked, until the day when something goes wrong and everything blows up in your face. Your staff need regular and potent doses of encouragement and motivation from you if they are to maintain a sense of achievement in the face of management who may take them for granted one day and complain bitterly the next.

SIGNS OF A LACK OF COMMITMENT

You can always tell when a department lacks motivation. The commonest symptoms are high absenteeism and sickness levels. Typically, these occur on Fridays or Mondays, or the days before or after public holidays. Poor timekeeping is another sign, showing that people do not consider their work matters enough for them to get there on time. People will leave on the dot of five, saying that they have to meet someone or get to the shops before they close. The prospect of their volunteering to work overtime – or to do anything else for that matter – is remote in the extreme.

Another way you can notice a lack of commitment is when people create unnecessary difficulties about the job. Their attitudes have become so rigid that they are prepared to do only what they are asked to do, and only in the way they are asked to do it. They exhibit a divorce of hands from minds, and activity becomes automatic and mindless. An important side-effect of this is that the quality of work suffers, and productivity falls, causing morale to fall still further. People feel that nobody will notice if they cut corners and that nobody is measuring output.

The 'us and them' syndrome is another hallmark of a lack of commitment. A secretary in the head office of a large high street retailer was overheard by her boss saying 'They've got some lovely green scarves in the Bromley store'. Her boss in turn asked: 'Who are "they"?'

MOTIVATING THE TEAM

A great deal can be achieved in the way of motivation simply in the everyday running of the department. Always be aware of the contributions your team can make, even to your own job. Sharing responsibility and feedback with you will in itself create a sense of commitment.

Motivation by involvement

When you are promoted to supervisor, without realising it you become 'one of them', the hierarchy of the organisation which separates you from those you used to work beside. Although this may be a sobering thought, it is important to try to minimise the distinction by emphasising the part played by the team. You can do this far more easily than you might think, by using the words, 'us', 'we' and 'our' as often as you can.

If you are choosing new furnishings for the office, ask for suggestions about colour schemes and take people along with you to exhibitions or furniture showrooms to try chairs for size and comfort. You'll find it useful to take the tallest and the shortest, on the premise that if the furniture suits them it will suit everyone else in between those sizes. Include subordinates in user group meetings, so that they feel they are making a genuine contribution to the changes taking place. You will not be the first supervisor who has been surprised at the high quality of their suggestions.

Ask people's opinions and advice, and try to take their advice even if you know it won't work. If you constantly reject ideas you will never have the kind of atmosphere you need, in which people's ideas flourish and contribute to the team's sense of commitment. The supervisor sets the tone of the section or department, and consulting people is an excellent way of creating an exciting climate where creativity thrives.

Motivation by delegation

Delegation is an art practised only by people who are self-confident and potentially successful. It is the skill of giving to a subordinate the responsibility for a part of your job, while you retain the overall accountability. Because this particular high-wire is fraught with so many dangers, most people delegate far less than they should. As a result they themselves are overworked, and their staff feel that they are not considered competent to take on more responsible work.

The first danger is that the job will not be done properly, so you need to take a lot of trouble to ensure that proper instructions are given and that these are clearly understood. As communicator, you are accountable if someone fails to understand you. Some people fear that a subordinate will learn to do the job better than the delegator. Of course this can happen, but wise supervisors accept the fact that they are not necessarily the best person at every job. On the other hand, you should take care that you are delegating the right job to the right person. If you make a mistake here, you run the risk of lowering your subordinate's sense of achievement because the job was too much to cope with.

Far more significant than the dangers, however, are the advantages of delegation. It gives your subordinates freedom of action, enabling them to get on with the job without interference from you. You should do all you can to resist the temptation to meddle, though you need to keep a close, tactful eye on things.

When you delegate, you give people a greater sense of involvement with the organisation because you are raising the level at which they operate. Some supervisors try to tell their staff that they have every confidence in them without ever putting the thought into action. Delegation is a way of doing just that: a way of saying in practical terms that you think this or that person is entirely capable of doing a job more complex and responsible than the one they are doing at present.

You may be tempted to think that your staff already have enough to do, and this is often an excuse given by managers who want to keep their cards close to their chests. A clerk in a shipping company who was put in charge of minuting the staff consultative committee willingly gave up two lunchtimes a week in order to write up the notes neatly and accurately. Delegation gives a better quality of work, greater interest and more variety, and it rarely fails because of lack of time. When people have interesting jobs they make time for the job because they want to do it.

Delegation is one of the best ways of training staff and developing skills they did not realise they had. It is also an excellent way of freeing your own time to learn parts of your boss's job which you may need to master for the future. What, you may ask, can I delegate? Try delegating responsibility for maintenance of stationery supplies, highlighting the difficulties the department had when you last ran out of printer paper or ribbons. Ask your staff to keep records of the consumption of each item, and suggest to everyone ways in which you might be able to save money by cutting down. For example, it is very extravagant if the information on data input forms is inaccurate. They have to be done again, time is wasted and so are the forms themselves.

You can delegate holiday charts to someone, making sure that they check that the department is adequately covered during peak work periods. Some supervisors delegate the reading of the technical press to a subordinate, asking them to look out for particular items of specific interest: other users of your equipment, new products which might help keep the equipment cleaner, or new information on health and safety when working with VDUs.

You can try delegating someone to look after new staff. You retain accountability for proper induction of new personnel, but you share the load. One seventeen-year-old facing her first supervisor was terror-struck to find herself at the mercy of someone who appeared at least as old as her grandmother. Fortunately, the supervisor had appointed a 'shepherdess' in the form of another teenager, who could relate better to the newcomer and shadow her until she had found her feet.

Efficiency and monitoring

Delegation is a useless exercise unless you keep tabs on what is going on. You need to make regular checks and ensure that all other staff concerned know who has been delegated which job. If, having delegated, you abandon your staff to their own devices, don't be surprised if disaster follows. You cannot abdicate accountability for any part of your job, and it is an important part of the job to be efficient and organised. Perhaps you thought efficiency was just for secretaries, but you would be quite wrong.

If you have ever worked for an inefficient boss, you will know how frustrating it is to have someone ask you to do things, and then never ask about them because they have no adequate follow-up system. If you ask someone to do a job for you and then just leave it, you will find that the next time you ask they will take on the task with a marked lack of enthusiasm and commitment. Because you have established a precedent of not checking back, the quality of the work will suffer too.

When you supervise an automated office, you are much more closely dependent on other departments and on the DP specialists than you were before. There are more precise deadlines to be met and far greater chaos will result if you fail. Your efficiency will act as an example and a motivator to your staff, and will give them a standard to work to.

Many supervisors seem nervous of setting standards of accuracy and efficiency. If you value the output and quality of the work your section does, it is your job to make sure your staff know what you expect. If you want the office kept tidy, and desks cleared every evening, you should say so. Remember, though, to set a good example. Setting a good example is not all there is to leadership, but it is a very important aspect of it. If you do one thing and insist on others doing something different, you deserve the problems you will get.

Letting people get on with the job

You should not really have time to be breathing continually down the necks of your staff, but this does not mean that you should not know what is going on. When you have new staff, you need to keep a careful eye on them, whether or not you have delegated the 'shepherding' task to someone else. One lad of nineteen went to work in the despatch department of a large building supplies company. Asked how he was getting on at the end of the third week, he said 'Terrific! I'm on my own next week — my boss is going to a trade show.' If you treat people like competent adults, they nearly always behave sensibly.

When you leave people to get on with their work, though, do look out for signs that they have hit trouble. Look for piles of paper where other people have cleared their desks. Look for worried faces and people who seem to be avoiding you. If staff have not understood your instructions first time, they will be reluctant to come back for a second or third explanation.

Thanking people and sharing praise

Your staff are probably coping heroically with a complex and confusing change in procedures. They need encouragement when things get tough, and they deserve praise when they have achieved some-thing worthwhile. Be careful not to overdo the praise, however, because you can so easily devalue the coinage.

When you have reached a difficult stage in the computerisation of your office, and things are going well, you will find it very worthwhile to say 'Thanks' to the team, perhaps even taking them out together to celebrate a successful month or at the end of a difficult week when you have had to cope and get the work out in spite of an epidemic of 'flu. If you are going out for a team celebration, organise it at a round table if you can: you will be surprised at the effect this has on bringing the team together.

When your own boss tells you how pleased everyone is with the performance of your department, it is churlish not to share the praise with the rest of the team. You will enjoy the praise more yourself, too. Sometimes it is helpful to chart the achievements of your own department and compare them with others. Make sure you identify achievements and successes. These are tremendous team motivators, and nothing succeeds like success. When you have something really worthwhile to celebrate, encourage everyone to join in to show how you value everyone's contribution.

MOTIVATING THE INDIVIDUAL

Motivation is more than a question of sharing responsibility. Your staff need to feel that they are valuable members of the company, both through knowing what they are helping the company to achieve and through being aware of their own potential.

Valuing individual contributions

It is surprising how often people working in offices do not clearly understand the corporate objectives of their organisation. People frequently describe their own jobs as being 'just' or 'only': 'I'm just the person who checks the reps' expenses', they say, or 'we're only input clerks'. Everyone's job is important and everybody has a vital part to play in the day-to-day running of an organisation and a department. Your staff should all have job descriptions which should be a list of the responsibilities of the job-holder, together with the tasks they need to carry out to meet those responsibilities. Everyone's job description should include personal targets which are intended to encourage their development in the job.

Your job as supervisor includes responsibility for making sure that everyone knows just how important their part is in the overall scheme of things. In addition to this, people need to know how their department fits into the total corporate strategy.

This means that you must make yourself thoroughly familiar with the organisation's objectives, and be able to explain them to your subordinates. Suppose your company is tendering for a large contract overseas, and wins that contract on price margins. It is essential for you to tell your staff that the cost reductions produced by computerisation were an important factor in enabling the company to offer such a competitive price. This, more than anything else, brings home to them the importance of the contribution made by your department.

If your department sends out invoices to customers, you will be familiar with the customer who refuses to pay when an invoice reflects small errors. Each time this happens, you involve the company in another month's credit to the customer with corresponding bank overdrafts. Accurate invoicing can, in this way, be precisely measured so that people understand the actual cost to the company of careless data input.

Many organisations produce an Employee Report annually. This is not a report on each worker, but a version of the annual Report and Accounts which can be readily understood by everybody, rather than just the company secretary. This document should be distributed to all staff and you should make sure everyone takes the trouble to read it. Then they can appreciate, for instance, how the rates paid by their company have contributed to the building of a new hospital or school which is part of the community.

Showing people the end product

There are other ways of letting people feel they are making a worthwhile contribution. Make sure each member of your staff knows about and can identify with the products or services which your organisation provides, and the customers or clients they provide them for. Tell them where your raw materials come from, and what political or climatic factors affect the work pattern. If, for example, your staff are checking computerised stock control in the timber business, you will find there are work peaks in May and October. This is the time when the Baltic and the St Lawrence thaw and freeze respectively, releasing or blocking your vital raw material supplies.

One large engineering company, working on a government contract, received a visit from staff from the appropriate ministry, who wanted to thank personally the word processing operators who were typing the manuals on the use of the equipment. Subsequently, the supervisor and operators were invited to visit the finished project, which included seeing their manuals in use. If people cannot visualise the end result of their work, and cannot identify their part in it, they can hardly be expected to show a sense of commitment in trying to achieve it.

If you know someone has started a project, make

sure they know how it all turned out, even if they are now working on something quite different. The data entry clerks of a large pharmaceutical company were asked what their organisation had done that they felt most proud of. Seven out of ten mentioned the success of a new product, a pre-emergence herbicide, which had been launched the previous summer. The training manager was astonished – and delighted – to know that staff at that level had taken such an interest in such a technical area.

Taking an interest in the individual

Without prying into people's private lives, it is part of your job to know how they are getting on at home, whether they have passed their driving test, where they are going on holiday. If someone has serious illness at home, try to be relaxed about timekeeping, and ask about the person who is ill. You will very seldom find people taking advantage of you and coming in late. Much more likely they will work extra hard, building up a 'bank balance' of goodwill in case there comes a time when they have to take time off for domestic reasons.

Taking an interest in individuals of course includes appraisals at regular intervals so that they know how they are getting on. Even at irregular intervals, if the occasion warrants it, you can ask people into your office just to tell them how delighted you are with their performance. They may think they are doing fine, only to discover that you expected far greater things of them. One manager decided to hire a new DP supervisor because the one in post was not 'measuring up'. Discussion of the problem highlighted the fact that the existing supervisor had no job description and probably thought she was doing very well.

Appraisals are, for most people, an annual event, and an opportunity to look back over past achievements and to identify the next steps in someone's career. Companies who neglect appraisal run the risk of severely demotivated staff who may never find out whether they are doing what you want them to do. Some managers say that they speak to their staff when they have done something wrong, to pull them back into line. This is about as useful as setting out on the M1 for Birmingham and continually seeing signs for Cornwall or Canterbury. This does not mean that you should not speak to people when their poor performance or behaviour merits it. In fact, a supervisor who evades discipline is heading for a rocky future. Appraisal is a chance to set down a person's strengths, problem areas, successes and future training needs.

Training for commitment

The word 'training' is sometimes its own worst enemy. Many people are quite offended when you mention it, since the implication is that they (still) don't quite know how to do the job. When you are working with computers, VDUs and changing software, training becomes absolutely essential for everyone on an ongoing basis: it is not a one-off, like baptism. Although the subject is dealt with in some detail in Chapter 8, it is relevant here because it is in itself a powerful motivator.

Training people is a way of saying to them that you think they have sufficient potential to warrant the department spending time and money on improving and building on their skills. No organisation is going to invest in training people who can never benefit from it. Most people recognise that this would be simply another way of throwing good money after bad, but some still may feel that it is an exercise in remedying totally unsatisfactory performance.

Courses should be selected with care, and any reputable training organisation will spend time advising you on what courses are appropriate for which staff. You should always brief people before they go, reminding them of the purpose of the course, and debrief them on their return, asking them to report on the course and to tell you what they can do as a result of the course that they could not have done before. One seventeen-year-old in his first office job had the thrill of his life when his boss told him that he was sending him on a computer programming course: suddenly he felt like someone who really mattered.

Target-setting

Target-setting sometimes depresses people. They see the target as an unattainable goal and convince themselves that they will never achieve it. Some see targets as trip-wires or obstacles. The way some managers set targets, you can understand the fear they can create. The purpose of target-setting is to give people an opportunity to develop their talents in a positive direction and in line with the job they are doing. Targets should be included in job descriptions, and should be updated annually.

Targets are the means by which you stretch people beyond the limits they think they are capable of reaching, and you should try to set realistic targets, such as:

● Learn to act as relief operator on a new piece of equipment.
● Learn to write a computer program.
● Visit computer shows and bring back recommendations for cheaper low-cost entry

equipment for word processing.
- Learn and explain to others the computer jargon currently in use.
- Spend a week or more on an exchange visit to the DP department.
- Update the procedures manual in line with new software releases.
- Attend and report on supplier/user group meeting for your department.

The interesting point about target-setting is that, if you run out of ideas, you can ask your subordinates for ideas of their own. Nine times out of ten they will set themselves far more demanding targets than you would have dared to suggest yourself. They will probably achieve them too. One final point on target setting: make sure that all the targets are not set to mature at the same time. Targets should have a time set for them and, if you are not careful, you will precipitate a desperate rush at the end, with correspondingly lower standards of achievement.

Developing people's social skills

When people do jobs which threaten to become monotonous, it is surprising how they retreat into themselves, losing self-confidence and turning into ineffective communicators, unable to express themselves or stand up for their viewpoints. Clerks who have no opportunity to talk to staff beyond their own departments very soon lose the habit of speaking up for themselves, and even seem to go out of their way to avoid talking to other staff in extreme cases.

If you can develop your staff's social skills, you will not only encourage their own commitment, but you will also create a department of cheerful, self-confident and communicative people. In this way you benefit as well, because the rest of the organisation is bound to notice the aura of activity your staff will generate.

Clerks should be able to deal directly with customers, clients or suppliers, so that they feel a part of the larger world beyond their work stations. This is particularly important in very large organisations, where the sheer size of the company can create 'tunnel vision' – people lose sight of anything beyond the company. This can be especially acute where the offices are geographically isolated and employees' only journeys are from home to office by company bus or their own cars. Shift workers are prey to this, too, because they tend only to mix with other people who work similar shift patterns. Dealing direct by phone or letter with customers encourages skills of communication, and it also gives people a greater feeling of responsibility. A customer who is not satisfied knows exactly who to ask for next time, so there is a greater impetus to provide satisfactory service.

Staff whose jobs are repetitive can be put in charge of other things, as with a Kent company who put one of their data preparation staff in charge of the firm's annual charity collection. This included representing the company at the charity's local social events and reporting back to the staff who had made donations, telling them what their money had been used for and explaining future projects.

If your organisation has a sports and social club, encourage people to join it and, if possible, to get involved in things like the darts competition or a cricket match against another local company. Suggest that people get together to organise the department's Christmas outing. Many people have untapped skills and if you fail to make use of these talents you will not profit from them, and your staff will find them becoming rusty. The bonus is added commitment because you have asked people to do something they are good at, and presumably like doing, and the team benefits from the use of these skills.

Communicating for commitment

A great many of the things you can do to gain greater commitment involve effective and systematic communication with your staff. This is handled in detail in Chapter 5. To be effective as a motivator you need to communicate in an organised way, and people deserve better management than mushrooms, being kept permanently in the dark.

GAINING PEOPLE'S COMMITMENT: A SUMMARY

The essence of gaining commitment is for the supervisor to make sure that people know what they are supposed to be doing, why they are doing it and where they fit in the overall pattern of the organisation's structure and objectives. The supervisor needs to be sure people know how they are doing, how they can improve, and what training is available to them. People generally thrive on responsibility and will give you extra commitment in helping you to get the job done.

Case Study: Retail Butcher

This is a small company, selling meat on a retail basis in a small village. It is owned and run by the family which started the business, and they are keenly aware of the potential jobs which could be created if the business ran successfully and expanded.

In the late 1970s, it became apparent that the introduction of a microcomputer could bring time and cost-saving benefits to the company. The structure of the company did not allow for complex departmental organisation, and each individual was expected to be accountable for their own work quality. The director felt that microcomputers would be an excellent way of doing this.

The main benefit would, it was hoped, be the saving in time and cost. There would be added benefits in being able to provide customers with more up-to-date information and this was expected to improve public relations. Not that the company's PR image was not good: the director felt it would further enhance it by being seen to be a go-ahead company.

For the staff themselves, the benefits would lie in increased motivation, resulting from successfully operating the equipment which would show everyone quickly and accurately how they were doing.

The director approached The Industrial Society for help because he could find no software suitable to the company's needs. The Society suggested that the company approach a nearby university where students were known to be looking out for project work as part of their computer studies courses.

Although the university felt that the company were ahead of their time, they readily agreed to undertake the project. They had found it difficult to raise interest in local companies, yet as an institution they were very keen to establish and maintain links with industry and commerce, to ensure that they were training their students in the skills which would be in demand when they graduated. For the company's part, the director was delighted to feel he was making a contribution to the community.

At this stage, while the students were working on the project, the director began including the micro project in his regular briefing of staff. Because he was himself enthusiastic and committed to the scheme, he was able very successfully to communicate the benefits to his staff. He was able to relate the details to people's jobs. For example, the company would be able to plan ahead better because they could project customers' needs based on their orders over the previous twelve months. The staff could immediately see the benefits and relevance of this, as it would reduce waste from over-ordering, and enable them to approach customers to remind them of their past orders and consumption. This, in turn, created a feeling of extra confidence in the company's ability to keep track of its affairs, and those of its customers.

There was still the question of the attitudes of micros among the people who would operate them. Bearing in mind the fact that they lived in an environment which was somewhat distant from computers, the director sent the office staff to evening classes to increase their understanding of microcomputers. Of course, they also met people from other companies and widened their horizons considerably.

The briefing meetings continued, the director outlining the progress of the project and explaining each stage as it occurred.

Some problems, of course, arose. These were particularly acute with the hardware; in its way, this was fortunate. The staff who had been accustomed to operating meat cutting equipment were familiar with the problems of mechanical failures. On occasions when the hardware caused problems, such as printer failures, the meat cutters were entirely sympathetic because they had experience of similar difficulties themselves. This prevented another common phenomenon in business: the gulf between office and shop floor. Each understood the other's problems, when they arose.

Up to the present, this small business has used microcomputing for stock control and customer records. The next stage is the computerisation of accounts, and a study is now in progress to evaluate the needs of the future. Because the director had communicated his own commitment and enthusiasm to his staff all along the way, he retains sufficient motivation. to encourage suggestions from staff as they progress. There remain small problems of frustration with hardware, which are probably average for any business.

By and large, however, all the staff feel proud to belong to a company which, five years ago, took a step into the unknown. As a result of this, they feel confident and knowledgeable on a subject which still baffles millions. And, of course, the company has grown and created more jobs which, to a certain extent, was the original objective.

7 Health and safety

The greatest danger to health associated with VDUs is management attitudes which fail to provide adequate working conditions. Since the Health and Safety at Work Act of 1974 there has been a sharp increase in the amount of attention paid to people's working conditions. In certain areas, such as farms and factories, this consideration has always played a major role in the job of the person in charge. Offices, however, have largely escaped scrutiny until well into the 'seventies, when the influx of VDU-based technology focused attention on the whole complex subject of office working conditions. Ergonomics, that is the relationship between people and their working conditions, is now an important aspect of any office supervisor's job when work is done on screens instead of paper.

Most organisations employ a specialist safety officer who will normally be available for expert advice and guidance. In practice this is not enough because the daily detail of working with VDUs may well be beyond the safety officer's experience. Supervisors at the sharp end need to have a well-informed approach to health and safety so that they can see for themselves that improvements are carried out correctly when needed. They also need to keep a lookout for potential risks and dangers. This chapter covers the areas where supervisors need to have detailed specialist knowledge.

VDUs AND EYESIGHT

Without a doubt, the subject of eyesight has been the first topic of real concern in electronic offices. There have been reports, often magnified by the non-specialist press, which predicted all manner of dangers to eyesight. The truth of the matter is that, including the paper published by the Health and Safety Executive in June 1983, no organisation has yet been able to produce scientifically-based data which prove that VDUs damage eyesight. On the other hand, there is no evidence that VDUs do eyesight any good.

Eyestrain

Eyestrain is a very common complaint among operators, especially during the early days of an installation. The first point to remember is that people are being asked to make radical changes in their work patterns. Instead of paper or a typewriter, they are looking at a screen which has been placed at an unfamiliar work angle. Eyes need time to adjust to a screen which flickers, and which usually displays characters and formats in a strange layout. VDUs are larger than most earlier office equipment. Operators need to move their heads and eyes more so as to make sure they are using the correct function keys. If their previous work has not been done on a VDU, they will only be accustomed to looking at paper set up on their left or right hand side, and will normally take only a quick glance at the keyboard, calculator, input forms or whatever.

In many cases the QWERTY keyboard will be a totally new concept, though ex-secretaries will have the edge here because they know the keyboard so well. It is worth remembering, though, that most secretaries are very hesitant on non-alphabetical keys because there has never been a standardised layout for commas, ampersands, brackets etc. They will almost certainly be unfamiliar with function keys.

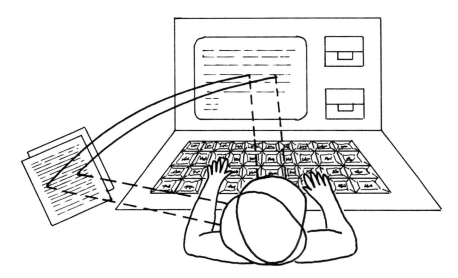

Figure 7.1   Eye motion between the screen and documents on the desk

The result of all this will be an increase in the movement of heads and eyes, which will cause the eyes to move over a wider arc than previously (see Figure 7.1). Operators may be working from a document holder which, on its stand, will be at virtually the same level as the screen; this arc of vision will be small and should not cause strain. Working from a document holder does not remove

the need for a look at the keyboard now and again,
but this arc will be longer and shallower than the

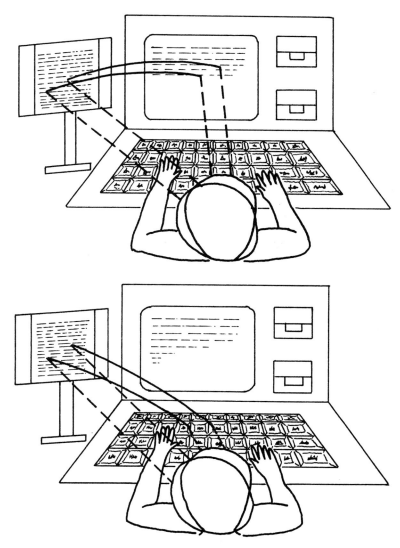

**Figure 7.2   Eye motion when using a document
holder on a stand**

document-to-screen arc. Figure 7.2 illustrates this.

The distance from eyes to document should be the same as from eyes to screen. This reduces the frequency with which eyes need to refocus, in turn reducing fatigue.

Where work is being read off papers laid out to the side of the operator, the eyes will still need to travel over a wider arc than in the past, because most terminal keyboards are larger than conventional typewriter keyboards.

Much of the mythology of eyestrain stems from the incorrect assumption that people using keyboards look at the screen all the time. Only in the early days after installation will operators look very frequently at their screens, apprehensively examining it to check that what they thought would appear on the screen is actually there. During normal work, the only type of worker who will spend long periods looking at the screen is the audio-typist working at a word processor, though some audio-typists say they do not actually look much at the screen. In any event, if you are the supervisor you should check carefully to make sure that people do not spend over-long periods at the screen without a break. The subject of rest breaks is dealt with in a later section of this chapter.

Eyestrain is a function of change at work and when operators complain of eyestrain there may be a multitude of causes, most of which have very little to do with operating a VDU, and a great deal to do with the exercising of lazy eye muscles and the normal apprehension felt in a strange working situation. People who feel stiff after riding a horse for the first time do not normally blame the horse as a hazard to health. Some opticians actually argue that this exercising of the eye muscles improves muscle tone rather than the reverse.

Deterioration of vision

Eyesight deteriorates for a wide variety of reasons,
few of which can be blamed on technology in the
office. In the late teenage years, and up to the age of
about twenty-five, eyesight can alter quite markedly,
and with surprising speed. The significance of this is
that many operators fall within this age bracket and
you need to bear in mind the associated psycho-
logical and emotional development of young people
which takes place during this maturing period.
Teenagers can need changes in their glasses as often
as three times in a year, quite apart from any
unproven effects of VDUs.

At the other end of the age range the problem is
more acute. Teenagers have normally had an eye test
on entry to secondary education, but older operators
will not often have had this check. Eye testing has
not always been a regular part of school life, and
vision can deteriorate gradually over a long period
without the person being aware of it.

It is estimated that over 70 per cent of people over
the age of forty have uncorrected visual defects of
one type or another. This is the age at which some
people need to start wearing glasses for the first time
in their lives. Whether for reasons of vanity or not,
many people are put off any action until the
shortness of their arms forces them to the optician
for a check-up!

Bear in mind, too, that each of us sees in our own
way. We have no yardstick by which to measure our
own, or anyone else's vision. We generally assume
that what we see is exactly the same as what
everyone else sees, and many of us would be wrong.

The difficulty for operators in the 40+ age range
who already wear glasses is that bifocal glasses will
cause problems. Typically, bifocal wearers will bob

their heads up and down, trying to decide which part of the lens gives better vision of the screen. In turn, this will produce complaints that VDUs cause aching necks.

A further complication is that, during this age range of 40 to 50, the difference between long and short distance vision will often change markedly. If operators are working with the wrong type of glasses they will have to refocus the eyes constantly, which will emphasise fatigue and stress. Their work output will also fall because older eyes refocus more slowly, which increases the time taken to read input data.

Arranging eye tests

A great many organisations arrange eye tests for operators before they start working on VDUs. Some also continue this with six-monthly or annual check-ups. This safeguards the employer from the charge that the VDU was the cause of deterioration in vision, rather than some of the natural causes described above.

Under the NHS, everyone is entitled to one free eye test a year from the optician of his/her choice. As an employer, you should arrange for operators to have eye tests carried out by a company-appointed optician. If you simply send them along to their own optician, they may reasonably complain that they will have to pay for another check-up if they need it within the year.

Most employers do in fact send operators to a company optician, who then reports back to the company. It is essential that the optician you choose has a clear understanding of the type of work to be done and the technology involved in doing that work. The Association of Optical Practitioners issues a professional guideline which explains very clearly the nature of this type of eye test, including a checklist for the examining optician. A good optician will also ask to see the office where the operators will be working. There are bound to be factors which the employer will overlook, but which may be highly significant to the optician.

Some operators may well end up needing glasses, and many employers will pay all or part of the cost of these. As one personnel manager in an oil company said: 'It's our work we are asking them to do: we have a moral obligation to provide them with the correct tools for the job.' A great deal of attention is paid to these matters in Scandinavia, and the Danish Employers' Federation recommend their members to pay for special working glasses where needed.

Preventing problems

Screens

Most VDUs have screens with green characters on a dark grey background, but other colours are also available: for example, light grey on dark grey and vice versa, though the dark grey actually looks as though it is black. Some operators use orange on brown and are very enthusiastic about this particular combination.

The size of the characters on the screen is important, and you should take care that it is easy to read. A great many screens show type in dot matrix characters, which should be a minimum size of 5×7, that is five dots across and seven down. Anything with fewer dots than 5×7 gives very poor character definition and is extremely difficult to read quickly.

Characters should be at least 3 mm high and spaced so as to make reading easy. Space between lines should be a minimum of 2 mm and character spacing is ideal at 10 to 12 pitch, that is 10 to 12 characters per inch.

Screens showing characters in capitals only should be avoided. Reading on these screens is very difficult, and proof-reading even worse. This is because the eye scans text and reads by letter shapes, rather than picking its way through a word letter by letter. Motorway signs are a good example of this, where one has a fraction of a second to distinguish between Birmingham and Burton-on-Trent. The latter has no descenders, which makes it easier to identify.

Descenders are the loops or tails on letters such as g, j, p, q and y. Ascenders appear in b, d, h, l and t. These should be clearly defined on the screen for faster, more accurate reading and lower levels of operator frustration.

To reduce the tiredness which sometimes results from screen flicker some operators turn down the brightness control when inputting large amounts of text or data, and only turn it up again when checking work for accuracy. It is an important part of the supervisor's responsibilities to ensure that these contrast controls are always in good working order. It is very easy for an operator to become accustomed to a gradually deteriorating contrast and not to notice it. By regularly Walking the Job, being on site, and using each operator's terminal now and again, supervisors can spot and correct malfunctioning equipment far better than regular users.

Most screen finishes are now matt, which makes for lower reflection, but if you have an older-type terminal you can buy a screen filter which produces a matt finish and can be removed for cleaning.

All VDU operators should clean their screens daily: if your operators are trying to work through layers of dust and smeary finger marks they will be significantly less productive and probably more irritable than colleagues with clean screens. Screens should always be adjustable so that the operator looks at it from an angle of about 40° below the normal horizontal line of vision. Controls for adjustment should be easy to operate, and should be placed within easy reach of the operator. Any difficulty in reaching controls will act as a deterrent to use. The recommended distance from the tip of the nose to the screen is 55 cm (about 22 inches).

Lighting

In an attempt to provide the best possible conditions of work for VDU operators some employers go overboard and create an environment where operators feel they need dark glasses. The fact is that gentle lighting is far better than the harsh effect created by fluorescent tubes. Many offices use uplighting, which has the effect of throwing light upwards on to the ceiling, which in turn reflects the light downwards on those working below. The result is much softer than fluorescent lighting, since there are fewer shadows and dark corners. Uplighting also gives a more restful atmosphere. Fittings for uplighting can be free-standing on the floor or wall-mounted.

If your office does use fluorescent lighting, the tubes should be protected by a diffuser which softens the light. Ideally, when operators look up from their terminals they should be looking at the strip light end-on, rather than broadside-on. They should not work with their backs to windows, because of the reflection which results. For general use, 300–500 lux is the recommended level of brightness.

Where operators feel the need, you should provide individual task lighting: desk lamps with flexible necks would be ideal. They are available from high-street retailers and some clip on the edge of the desk, to save space.

Sunshine

If your office has outside windows, you will need blinds to prevent direct sunlight from causing glare. This is especially harmful if you have shiny screens. Many offices use horizontal Venetian or vertical Roman blinds to counteract this glare. These have the disadvantage of reflecting their own slats back on to the screen. The ideal, seldom seen, are rattan roll-up blinds which have such narrow individual strips that they merge on reflection to form what appears to be a smooth surface.

Office decor

Office walls should always be matt finished, to reduce reflection, and the addition of fabric screens creates a softer, warmer atmosphere. The objective is to try to offset the somewhat clinical appearance of some offices which can make people feel that they are working on a production line. Wall colour is not a major issue, but pale colours do give a feeling of great calm and spaciousness.

STRESS AND HEADACHES

You will always have the odd operator complaining of headaches, and the chances are that they will lay the blame at the door of management for introducing the new equipment. In fact, headaches are unlikely to have much connection with eyestrain or with the equipment itself. What is much more likely is that there is a connection between the changes associated with the introduction of new equipment. The installation of VDU terminals brings in its wake changes in seating patterns, new work practices, different forms to fill in and so on. These points are covered in more detail in Chapter 4. These, however, are the visible changes. The invisible changes are reflected in fear, tension, nervousness and 'not wanting to know'.

The same goes for updates on an old system: tension is not confined to the initial stages of computerisation, and it is quite predictable to suffer a headache as a result. Tension may also be aggravated by senior managements who expect instant results from new equipment or software (or both). This is an organisational problem associated with communication and is dealt with in detail in Chapter 5.

Where a system is the first step in computerisation it will normally form part of a dual system, operating in parallel with the old paper-based procedures. This will undoubtedly increase workloads, which will in turn increase the tendency towards headaches.

Headaches can also be caused by excessive noise, and relatively little attention has been paid to this. Most printers have acoustic covers but not all of these covers are as effective as they should be. Some companies build small soundproof rooms for their printers, but this is an expensive way of reducing the printer's clatter.

It is important to buy equipment in the right order. Many companies have bought printers without hopper or tractor feeds, only to find that their existing acoustic hood will not fit over the paper feed. The resulting alternative is either a new, larger hood or an intensely irritating noise.

THE WORKING ENVIRONMENT

While eyesight and headaches are the most obvious
health problems to tackle when working with VDUs,
the electronic office presents other risks to health
and safety which can be greatly reduced by sensible
office design and maintenance.

Office furniture

For many organisations office furniture is a
neglected area. Any old chairs, desks and tables have
too often been considered adequate, and the use of
electronic systems in the office has brought with it a
welcome change of attitude. Although many
organisations now buy purpose-built furniture, far
too many do not and the result is twentieth-century
equipment on nineteenth-century furniture.

Whether operators are using computer terminals
or word processors, they usually need to spend long
periods of time at the screen. This means that it is
doubly important to provide the right sort of chairs
for comfort and productivity. All chairs should be
fitted with five-star wheeled bases to enable the
operator to swivel easily to reach other work. Your
job as supervisor includes making sure that people
do not use these chairs to climb up on. If they need to
reach high shelves, it is better to invest in a 'toad-
stool' similar to those used for stacking shelves in
supermarkets.

Operators' chairs should have adjustable backrests
to allow both for personal preferences and for long-
waisted people. The height of the seat should be
adjustable, and it should always be possible for the
operator to rest both feet flat on the floor.

For short people, it is extremely uncomfortable to
have to spend all day with feet dangling and knees

hung over the edge of the seat. The veins at the back of the knee become severely pressurised and will cause considerable discomfort. This will particularly affect people with a tendency towards varicose veins, heart disease or other circulatory conditions. If you have operators shorter than about 5 ft 2 in, they can be given wedge-shaped footrests. There should be 20 cm clearance between the top of the seat and the table top to allow for easy movement of the thighs.

Operators' desks should provide sufficient space for paperwork: that is, space equivalent to a sheet of A3 paper on each side. This space is needed firstly for paperwork on which the operator may be working, and secondly for the manual which needs to be used opened out flat. (Most manuals are A4 size.) Desk tops should be non-reflective and should be about 70 cm (27½ inches) from the floor. More and more desks are being designed on a split-level principle, allowing the keyboard to rest in a recessed section. With older equipment, which has integrated screens and keyboards, this will be of little use, but most terminals are now designed with keyboards attached to the screen by means of a flexible cable. Desks should provide easy access to drawers, so that stationery can be kept dust-free: automated offices are surprisingly dusty places because of the static electricity.

Operators' chairs do not need arm-rests, which simply get in the way of smooth operation, but there is an increasing tendency to use palm-rests, which reduce fatigue in the upper arms. The chair should be near enough to the table that the operator does not have to work with outstretched arms for long periods. At the same time, it should not be so near as to have the operator's elbows extending beyond the line of the back.

Controlling the cabling

The installation of VDU terminals usually involves an attendant quantity of cabling which needs careful attention. Left to its own devices, cabling is unsightly and harbours dirt. Worse, it is a major hazard to passing traffic and should at all times be confined. There are several ways of doing this.

Some work stations carry plastic cradles which clip on the back of the work surface, keeping cables all together. Another way of controlling unsightly wires is to cluster them inside vertical ducting which has the advantage of breaking up the somewhat desert-like appearance of many open plan offices. These ducts need only be 3 in along each of their four sides. It is important, however, for staff to understand that such vertical ducting is not to be used for hanging calendars or as a support for trailing office plants.

Somewhat more costly, but arguably a better investment, is to lay wiring under the floor in much the same way as telephone cables are often laid. If your company is moving into an old building, you may well find that previous occupants have left wiring behind them and this should be cleared out to allow space for your new cables and wiring. Multiple outlet plugs can also be placed under the floor, so that when you decide to rearrange your office all desks will still be within easy reach of an outlet.

Power supplies

Many organisations arrange for 'clean' power supplies for their electronic equipment. Fluctuations in the public supply can cause a variety of problems ranging from severe screen flicker to loss of text or data.

By law, the public supply may only vary between 49.5 and 50.5 cycles. However, even minute surges of power can cause loss of text from the discs in use at the time. A bypass device will effectively protect computers from surges in the main supply and ensure that loss or damage to text or data is not caused by this means, although it is worth remembering that electricity surges are not the only causes of corruption of discs.

Static electricity

VDU terminals are well-known creators of static electricity which can give slight shocks to staff when they touch metal surfaces.

Anti-static sprays can be used, and a good rule of thumb is to spray four times a year, over a weekend to allow fumes to dissipate while the office is empty. Anti-static mats are also widely used, and come in many shapes and sizes.

Static electricity acts as a magnet to dust, and this is one reason why screens get dirty so quickly. People who use VDUs may not realise how often they touch their screens, pointing something out to someone else, for instance, or suggesting various ways of moving text on the screen. Every time a finger touches the screen, it leaves behind it a minute deposit of grease which in turn attracts yet another layer of dust. Some operators find that the static attracts dirt to their skin, which can cause rashes and pimples.

Air conditioning and ionisers

Almost all large computer installations – those with

round-the-clock mainframes – are air conditioned.
Not only does this reduce noise from outside, but it
also keeps the air cleaner and maintains a stable
working temperature in an environment where the
equipment itself may give off considerable amounts
of heat.

There is a body of opinion which holds that air
conditioning creates a harmful atmosphere,
encouraging headaches and dizziness, and this has
been attributed by some to an imbalance of negative
ions in the air.

Negative ions are minute electrically-charged
molecules which are typically found near beaches
and waterfalls, or in mountain areas. They are
attracted to airborne particles of dust and cigarette
smoke, as well as to metal surfaces and synthetic
fabrics. The effect of this attraction is to destroy the
negative ions and to produce an excess of positive
ions which, it is claimed, make people feel irritable
and tense.

To rebalance the atmosphere, negative ions can be
artificially replaced by fitting ionisers to ceilings or
having them free-standing on the floor.

The claims made for these ionisers are not
extravagant, and what documented evidence there is
is sound enough. However, they are not at present
very widely used.

Cleaning

Although automated offices generally give off an air
of hygienic efficiency, they are in fact remarkably
dirty places due to the static electricity which
positively encourages dirt. Keyboards should be
regularly cleaned, and screens should be wiped
daily. Products specifically designed for the purpose
are now available, although a paper tissue will do as

well. Light fittings should also be kept clean, since dirty fittings can cause light loss of up to 25 per cent of light available. It is essential that office cleaners are given crystal-clear instructions and reminders about what they should and should not touch, dust or unplug.

REST PERIODS

In the early days of automated offices, in the late 'seventies, many employers panicked at the suggestion that their staff should have work breaks. This was partly aggravated by the growing need for offices to increase their productivity by cutting down on coffee breaks, if not stopping them altogether. When the furore died down, it became apparent that most people already did take a break roughly every hour and a half, and that automation was simply focusing on something which had long been standard practice.

Some union initiatives in this area have specified that operators should take a break after forty minutes' work. The operators themselves quickly realised that they would hardly be able to get down to any serious work during this short period, and opted to work in spells of ninety minutes with roughly twenty-minute breaks for coffee.

With the phasing out of the formal coffee or tea break, many office workers spend large parts of their day consuming endless supplies of coffee and tea, but in an automated office this presents hazards which should be taken very seriously.

Firstly, there is a therapeutic benefit in getting away from the work station for a break, to exercise muscles which may become stiff, particularly across the shoulders. A few deep breaths and a short walk about do wonders in clearing the brain.

Secondly, there is a considerable risk of spillage of coffee, soup, yoghurt etc. You will, of course, have a maintenance contract with your supplier, but it is most unlikely to cover free repair work in cleaning out keyboards after such an accident. One case cited was of an operator who spilled lemonade on the terminal. Nothing happened for a few weeks, then suddenly a plume of smoke started coming out of the terminal causing considerable and understandable alarm. It had finally corroded due to the acid in the lemonade. The bill for this was £250.00.

Coffee breaks, then, are not a reflection of benign management but a practical way of saving money and maintaining productivity levels by keeping operators fresh and alert.

HEALTH AND SAFETY: A SUMMARY

Careful choice of furniture and lighting are essential to the smooth running of a productive automated office. Eye tests should be organised before starting VDU work, and thereafter annually. Air conditioning may be required for the control of temperature, dirt and external noise. Work breaks of fifteen or so minutes every hour and a half can save money as well as increasing productivity.

Office decor, cable housings and control of light sources from inside and outside are all part of the day-to-day responsibilities of the supervisor, and it is essential that information is kept up to date at all times.

8 Training your staff

For many supervisors, training seems to be the easiest part of the job – until they actually come to do it. Then, suddenly, it appears far more complicated than they expected, bits are left out, the trainee loses interest and the whole thing becomes a wearisome chore.

First, then, it is important to clarify the reasons for carrying out training at all, then to identify the people who need training. The problems will be analysed, and then there will be a suggested list of steps to go through, with comments on each.

WHY TRAIN?

As a way of reinforcing your leadership role training is hard to beat. Young people generally tend to respect and admire the people who taught them their jobs, and they usually remember them too, long after you have all moved to different parts of the company. It is an important motivator because nobody is going to spend time and money training people who cannot profit from it, and who are not and never will be suitable for promotion.

The third point is that training is an important

aspect of career planning. When they join companies many young people ask what career patterns they can expect. The answers they receive are not always very precise, and motivation slackens as a result. However, if you put the plan into action by training people to do specific jobs, each one further up the ladder than they are at the moment, they will place greater faith in your intention to carry out the plans you have on paper. Training for promotion can include a wide range of skills which are not always immediately related to the job in hand. For example, telephone and letter-writing skills are often sadly below standard, and the development of these talents will give staff the self-confidence to do a more complex job and to deal confidently with more senior staff, as well as outsiders such as clients, customers and suppliers.

When you want to move on to another job, you will need to have trained people to do your job before your boss will agree to your own promotion. In fact, the most promotable people are those who have delegated and trained their successors sufficiently well to enable their own promotion to take place very quickly, without their boss having to worry about leaving a massive hiatus in the running of the department. Bad delegators seldom get promoted.

If you have trained your staff effectively, you can go on holiday with a clearer conscience than if you are worrying about whether they will keep the place in order in your absence. You will not have to worry so much if you are off sick, either.

One manager in an engineering company went on holiday leaving some important tenders in his locked office drawers and taking the keys with him. It so happened that his own boss needed some of the tenders to check on the prices quoted, but could not gain access to the locked drawers. The prospective customer had queried something on the tenders, the boss was highly embarrassed, and the manager returned from his holiday to face more music than he would have wished.

You can expect a more productive department if people are properly trained, because you have greater flexibility when people are able to help out with jobs which they do not normally do. In addition, of course, the training will have acted as a motivator, bringing greater enthusiasm to those who are helping out.

WHO NEEDS TRAINING?

The short answer to this is 'everyone', and not just once, either. Training is an ongoing exercise, whether formal or informal. Your computer programs will surely not remain as they are for ever, and people need updating on that as well as on many other techniques.

Obviously your subordinates will need on-the-job training in the use of different terminals, new functions, redesigned forms and so on. New procedures may alter your workflow patterns, so people need to know how to cope with this. Ideally, you need to have a department in which everyone knows how to do everyone else's job. This covers you in time of illness, holidays or unavoidable crises. It is a mark of the successful supervisor that disasters seldom occur, because there is a contingency plan for virtually every eventuality. Life is never quite that simple but it is important to try and cover as many potential disaster areas as you can, which reduces the impact of these crises. Whether you call it 'learning from experience' or 'crisis prevention', you should aim to have an answer to every problem.

Besides training your subordinates, you need to think about training your superiors, especially in the use of word processing. Ignorance on the part of authors/users can play a significant part in making WP wasteful and expensive. They will need explanations of the jargon associated with WP, and they need to understand all the various functions available to them such as mail/merge, retrieving data from a variety of files to merge them into one document, stored formats, type styles, the time taken to print a page and so on. They also need to be reminded that all work still has to be keyboarded onto the WP in the first place, and that this is not much faster than on a regular typewriter. Some organisations produce an authors' guide which explains how the best use can be made of WP, but these need to be backed up by demonstrations on the equipment itself.

Remember four things:

- Managers will forget and need reminding.
- New staff will need training.
- Everyone will need updating.
- You won't win them all. There will always be the odd backslider who will send in nine or more versions of a draft.

In any event, once your department is computerised, the other departments in the organisation need to know what you are doing, what they can expect from you by way of faster services, and how their jobs fit in with your department's. Once people understand, their level of co-operation rises considerably and usually remains at that level.

Finally, do not forget training for yourself. Personnel departments do not always understand the training needs of computerised departments. Try to show your boss that you really do want to go on courses, and why. Write off for programmes, if need be, and talk them over with your boss, trying to highlight the benefits the organisation will receive if you go. It is better to do it this way than simply to ask your boss if you can go on a course. The best you get from this is a non-committal agreement and no further action. If you identify the course you think will help you most, you are reducing the amount of decision-taking your boss has to do, and you are showing a good deal of initiative in going to the trouble of sifting through the huge amounts of training material on the market.

If you can also cost out the exercise, to include travel, hotels etc., so much the better. Explain why you want to go on this particular course, and draw up a plan for the department to run smoothly while you are away for three days or so. Remember that if the course is some distance away you will have to leave the night before, and you may not reach home till the evening of the third day. It is often cheaper to stay in a hotel than to drive home each evening. In other words, do your homework and this will help convince your boss that you are serious, which will in turn bring a more positive response to you and your idea.

You should also help yourself to upgrade your skills by talking to reps, to find out what is new in the information technology world. Join professional organisations, like the British Computer Society or the Information and Word Processing Association. They are extremely useful for meeting people, swapping ideas, hearing how other people solve problems you may have and so on.

Above all, the trade press is an invaluable source of information about new products, new applications, job opportunities, salary scales, and information from the US and Europe which helps you to keep abreast of the pack, so to speak. Supervisors who have little technical knowledge and understanding make their own lives much more difficult than they need.

Do try to visit the trade shows, to keep up to date. There are now enough of these nationwide that nobody should find it impossible to go. Make a list before you set off of the things you want to see, put on comfortable shoes and go directly to the stands on your list. If you can plan your day in conjunction with the plan of the exhibition, you will save a great deal of time by arranging your tour in logical order, covering the shortest distance.

PROBLEMS OF TRAINING

There will always be difficulties in the way of the supervisor who wants to train staff. The first and most common problem is lack of time. This, translated, is an indication that you or your company do not think training sufficiently important to make time for it. If you are up against time pressure your training will be infinitely less effective, because your patience will diminish as you keep looking at your watch, thinking of all the other things you ought to be doing.

For many people cost is the main obstacle to training. This, too, is short-sighted, because training is one of the best investments which any organisation can make in the future of its employees. The analogy lies in saving for one's old age: somehow most of us manage to do it, because we think it is so important. The bonus from investing in training is not just that you get more competent staff: you also

Although the basic skills required for WP are the same as for typing, a certain amount of specialised training is needed to show operators how to use all the new facilities offered by word processing. Most manufacturers run their own training courses for customers' WP operators.

have more enthusiastic and committed people working with you.

Of course training interrupts your 'normal' flow of work, but this is only because you have not planned for it. Training is a part of your normal workflow. Many retail stores open half an hour late one morning a week to allow time for staff training, indicating that they are prepared to lose half an hour's takings for the sake of properly trained staff.

The reason why supervisors find training so difficult is probably that they know the job too well. The trick is to break the job down into small components, but this is easier said than done. Most people have heard the story of the driving examiner who asked a candidate what he should first do on getting into the car. The correct answer, which few people give, is 'Shut the door'.

PREPARATION FOR TRAINING

Identifying training needs

Before you start, it is essential to find out what your staff already know. There are various ways of doing this, but the best is simply to ask such questions as: 'Have you ever used a keyboard before?', or 'What kinds of VDU have you used?' You need to know what type of jobs they have had in the past: have they ever worked in a despatch department, for example, or a solicitor's office. Much of this information should be on their application forms or personal files, but make sure you check. Some people will be very fluent on the keyboard, perhaps if they have done signalling work in the services, so it is well worth asking about that, because they may not consider this experience as significant as you do.

These people will learn more quickly than 'search and peck' typists.

Figure 8.1 gives an outline of a simple training plan which you may find useful. Its chief virtue is its simplicity, as it highlights aspects of your department's work which you may have overlooked. Delegates filling in these plans on courses frequently get a sharp shock, finding out that they only have one person able to perform a particular function, or that someone else is badly under-utilised.

This is the type of situation which can easily explain, in part, a level of demotivation in people who have not enough to do. On the other hand, people who are able to do all parts of the job, and who appear bored, are probably ready for promotion. In the everyday rush of work, it is not easy to notice these things, and a simple format of this type can be extremely useful.

When you have successfully identified training needs you will probably have the answer to the question 'What do they need to know?', as opposed to what they already know. Training, then, is simply a matter of filling that gap, remembering that the whole training function is an ongoing process. As soon as they master one skill, they ought to be aiming towards the next, in an organised pattern drawing them on in the career direction planned.

Organising the time

Time for training does not just happen: it has to be planned, both in your own timetable and in the trainees'. You need to make sure that your boss and your department know what you are doing, and that you are not to be interrupted unless there is an emergency. Training sessions are ideally between

Names of Personnel	Insert/delete paragraphs	Move paragraphs	RH justification	Twin column transposition	Centring indented material	Paragraph merge	Footnote insertion	Duplicate page/text	Duplicate diskette	Back-up diskette	Address/letter merge	NOTES
Chris	×	×	×	×	×	×		×		×	×	Off sick frequently with backache
Pat	×	×	×							×		
Robin	×	×	×		×	×	×		×			
Bobby	×	×	×					×	×	×	×	Disruptive influence on the team: Started 20 March sit on her own?
Debbie	×											
Sue	×		×									Away sick 6 weeks
Carol	×											

Procedure:
1 List job headings.
2 List personnel.
3 Tick capabilities of each person.
4 Decide ideal capacity.
5 Consider personnel changes, performance standards and commitments.

Figure 8.1 A training plan to highlight jobs not adequately covered and people's individual workloads

one and two hours in length. If the session is less than an hour you cannot get properly involved in what you are doing, because the first ten minutes or so may be spent in revision work. Over two hours, the concentration span is exhausted and you will make little headway.

Preparing the equipment

It is humiliating, to put it mildly, if the equipment fails to work in a training session. It ruffles you and diminishes the confidence your trainee ought to have in you. So check everything before you start and, if you have time, check it again. Make sure you have to hand all the stationery, manuals, exercises etc. you need, as well as sample invoices, despatch notes, standard letters or whatever. Always have a spare pencil or two and, if coffee time falls within the training period, make a very clear break and move away from the keyboard. The point was made in Chapter 7 that coffee and tea should be drunk well away from terminals. Your training schedule may not fit neatly into this pattern, but set the example just the same: don't use the VDU and drink coffee at the same time. Make sure you have discs ready. If initialising is part of the training session, well and good, but if not, make sure your discs are already prepared for use. If you are training on a micro which is also used for word processing, make sure that nobody else is going to come and wait impatiently for you to finish your training session.

Preparing yourself

Before you begin a training session, make sure that you are properly organised. Ensure that you are totally familiar with the subject in hand, and that your mind is concentrated on it. Learning to operate a VDU is more complex than most people realise, and you need a clear head, particularly if you are training more than one person at a time. Many trainers use a 'crib sheet' as well as the manuals. Some manuals are extremely complicated and may be very off-putting to a beginner.

Don't ever be shy of using your 'crib sheet': the most effective way of doing it is to mark the keystrokes in capitals, putting a red box round them in felt-tipped pen. Beside them, in blue, write down the effect created by pressing that key. It's clear and simple. You may need to invest a good deal of time designing your 'crib sheets' but it will never have been wasted. Figure 8.2 shows an example.

Show and tell, or make them do it?

There are two schools of thought about how to train. One is that you should show trainees what you want done, do it again slowly and then get them to do it themselves. This runs the risk of terrifying people by making them think that they will never achieve such skill and fluency. On the other hand, it does show them what they are aiming at. The reverse idea is that you should explain the overall objective, and describe each step along the way towards achieving the goal. Which method you adopt depends on you and your student, and you may want to do it in different ways at different times.

Preparing the trainee

All trainees need basic information, such as what they are going to learn and how. It is particularly important to make sure that you motivate your student by pointing out what they will gain from the

Explain purpose of each part of equipment: keyboard, screen, disc drives, printer.

Keystrokes are in boxes for the student's use.

Command keys which appear *in the same boxes* should be pressed simultaneously.

Insert disc in Drive 1, label uppermost, print upside-down to user.

Close Drive 1 flap.

Switch on at left rear of consol, using rocker switch.

Explain the display which appears on the screen.

RETURN KEY	Serial number of program disappears.

Explain importance of cursor, its shape and function.

↓	Move cursor down.
↑	Move cursor up.
→	Move cursor right.
←	Move cursor left.
SHIFT	(creates > symbol) : Message: Go to co-ordinate, asking student for instructions.
A 1	
RETURN KEY	Explain that the Return Key executes the commands.
SALES	Explain that this is the student's own input.
RETURN KEY	
→	Cursor appears on next co-ordinate to right, ie B 1.
8000	Explain this figure, the only actual figure used in the exercise.
RETURN KEY	
← ↓	Cursor appears on co-ordinate A 2.
COSTS	Again, this is the student's own input.
RETURN KEY	
→	Cursor appears in B 2.
· 6 SHIFT : B 1	(creates .6 * B1) Explain relationship to figure in B 1.
RETURN KEY	
↓ ←	Cursor appears at left-hand margin, ie A 3.
PROFIT	More student input.
RETURN KEY	
→	Cursor appears on next co-ordinate to right, ie B 3.
SHIFT + B 1 − B 2	Explain purpose of + symbol: to differentiate between alpha and numerics for calculation purposes.
RETURN KEY	
↑ ↑	Returns cursor to B 1.
7500	Be sure the student watches while the alteration of this number automatically changes those relating to it.
RETURN KEY	

Figure 8.2 Example of tutor's training notes for a microcomputer spreadsheet program (eg Supercalc or Visicalc)

training, by highlighting the next stage they can move on to, or the new work they will be able to do. Success in training may also lead to promotion, so make sure you point this out.

THE TRAINING PROCESS

The school leaver

School leavers may form a sizeable percentage of the staff you need to train, besides those you train on various government training schemes. School leavers are not accustomed to doing the same thing all day, and may become easily bored. They may not have appreciated the implications of the word 'work' as opposed to 'a job'. They will be used to longer holidays and shorter working days than offices normally provide. They will be unfamiliar with their new position at the bottom of the ladder, after being head girl or captain of football. They will be used to instant rewards: full marks for good work, a system seldom found in offices. Other staff may expect miracles of them, not knowing that they are very new to the world of work. They will be very nervous and this will inhibit their learning processes. Training for young people is best done one-to-one, or one instructor to two students. The first prevents them from looking foolish in front of their peers, while the second allows them to encourage each other and practise with more commitment.

Established employees

These people probably know you and the organisation well, and there should not be any serious problems. In fact, it should be the easiest part of the training job. They will know the company jargon, abbreviations, personnel and so on, and will understand what the training is all about, especially since, by reading Chapter 4, you will have learned the importance of explaining change at work and the implications of this change for everyone's job. They will know what new skills they need to learn, and the savings in time and energy which will result. Further, of course, they will know you well since you will have been part of the working team for some time. As with school leavers, one-to-one or one-to-two is the best ratio for instruction, for much the same reasons.

Senior management

Training senior management members will present problems similar to those of the school leaver in that they will also be apprehensive, but for different reasons. They will be afraid of looking foolish if they are not able to understand what you are trying to explain to them. In contrast to the two previous learning situations, senior management are best taught in groups unless you are giving them individual keyboard skills on a micro, for example.

Senior management will most often need familiarisation with new systems, showing them the advantages to their departments of the new computerised data retrieval system. On word processing, they will have difficulty grasping some of the jargon of the keyboard. Terms like 'right-hand justification', 'underscoring' and '10 or 12 pitch' will be Greek to them, so be patient. They are unlikely to be familiar with the grammar and geography of the keyboard.

They need, and will want to know, the benefits which the new system will bring to their departments, so remember that your first task should be to point out the ways in which they will be better off by faster, more accurate work, quicker turn-round of reports, better information more easily accessible and so on. By all means tell them what the new system does, but do not confuse features with benefits. Features are what the system does; benefits are ways that people are better off by having work done faster, cheaper, more accurately.

If you can highlight particular bottlenecks in the past, so much the better, because you can use the same techniques as in Chapter 4, by pointing out that hold-ups will no longer occur, or will be solved more easily if they do. Try to explain things to your senior management in language they understand. Computer jargon will baffle and annoy them, and 'business English' will make you sound like someone you are not. If you mean 'get' don't use 'obtain': senior management are too busy to use long, meaningless words. Above all, make sure you convey to senior management the fact that you are not a computer 'boffin', and that anyone can understand how a computer or word processor works.

Be economical with their time at senior level. Invite them for a fifteen- or thirty-minute familiarisation session and make it just that. They have no time to waste, and their time is very expensive. If you can, have small groups at a time so that you can keep an eye on everyone and say, for example, 'Dr Jones, you look a bit puzzled: have I said something to confuse you?' Group pressure is very inhibiting and people will tend not to ask questions when surrounded by their peers. You may have to work to find out what is bothering someone, and one very good way to do this is to know as much as you can about the work each manager does, so that you can refer specifically to fears they may have by mentioning certain monthly reports etc.

You may think they ought to spend two or three days learning about the new system, but half an hour is probably the most they will be able to spare. Be glad they will spare it, make good use of the time, and thank them for coming. Be sure you make yourself freely available for questions during and after the session. Give proper status to a familiarisation session with senior management, by giving them coffee or tea, having the work area clean and tidy, and making it generally an occasion they will enjoy. It is a good ploy to invite your first batch of half a dozen or so from real enthusiasts. Then they will probably spread the word to their colleagues. Next time you issue an invitation you will have more enthusiastic acceptances. Face the fact that you won't win them all, but do use your admirers to act as your ambassadors.

What and why

Trainers rely on the three-times table: tell people what you are going to teach them, then teach it to them, and then tell them what you've just taught them. It forms an introduction, a middle and a summary, and gives trainees confidence in knowing what they have learned. Then they can tell others that they have learned to operate the stock control input forms, or the weekly despatch summaries or whatever. Always explain why each lesson is important. For example, it is important for accounts outstanding to be kept up to date so that letters can be sent to delinquent debtors. This speeds up the collection of debts, thus reducing the interest the company is paying on bank overdraft.

Some companies keep computerised records of company cars, complete with servicing records. If the garage rings to say that a certain car needs a new clutch, the computer records will show when the last clutch was fitted. If it was two weeks ago, the manager can refuse to pay for the latest clutch. If you can show this to a trainee, they can see at once how useful such a system is. Let them spend time going through all the records of company cars, and give you a list of those due for their MOT.

Keeping training records

It is important to keep a record of training done. A simple form such as the one shown in Figure 8.3 is all you need. Fill it in at the end of each session, and tell trainees at the beginning of their training that you are keeping these records. They will appear nervous for a moment, until you explain the purpose, which is to record each individual's progress for their personal file. It is good for them to be able to look back and see what they have achieved. For yourself, it is invaluable to keep a record of the people you have trained, for the time when your boss asks you what you have achieved this year. You should always keep records of the things you have done which you are proud of having achieved.

From a legal viewpoint, it is useful to have a record of having trained a person to do a particular job. Suppose you have to dismiss someone for incompetence. If you have a record of the training sessions during which you have tried to train that person to do the job, you should have no need to worry that you will come unstuck at an Industrial Tribunal. If, on the other hand, you cannot prove that you trained someone to do a job, it can be shown that their incompetence was partly your fault.

TRAINING RECORD

Name _____

Department _____

Disc name/code _____

Date of training session _____

Time of session _____

Work done

(a) Revision/review

(b) New work

Special difficulties

Tutor's initials

Figure 8.3   A training record form

Training at the keyboard

The first essential is to relax your student, in order to create complete confidence in you. Make sure your student knows what you mean by all the terminology, in particular hardware and software. Point out the various parts, for example the disc drives, consol, screen, printer. Don't be afraid of rote learning if it is appropriate. One of the advantages of one-to-one training is that you can use each person's catch-phrases for them personally. The odd joke goes a long way to easing any nervousness, and you should try to show your own enthusiasm for what you are teaching: enthusiasm is highly contagious.

It is vital to teach people, at a very early stage, proper and careful disc handling techniques. Discs should be inserted carefully, before the computer is turned on if you work on a microcomputer, to prevent the danger of damaging the disc by inserting it while the reader head is active. Similarly, after use, the terminal should be turned off before the disc is removed and replaced carefully in its protective envelope.

Always try to start by teaching something easy, so that people feel that they have achieved something worthwhile at an early stage. Make sure your student is comfortable, and has the correct glasses on. Check that the chair is the right height, including the back-rest, and get them to switch on the terminal so that they not only know where the controls are but also what they feel like. Get them to try out the contrast control so that they can adjust it to their own needs.

Be sure to tell people what noises the machine makes, and why. It is rarely anything to worry about, but people are bound to be alarmed at the odd 'beep'. Above all, of course, remind them that they cannot break the terminal or computer, short of dropping it on the floor or spilling liquids on it (see Chapter 7).

Explain only what you need to for each session: too much confuses so keep your enthusiasm under control. If your student is unfamiliar with the keyboard, sit on your hands rather than point out keys they are searching for. The element most often used may well be the space bar, which is rarely, if ever, marked as such, so make a point of highlighting it.

Many people find it very difficult to get the knack of using two keys simultaneously, as one would use the shift key and another key to obtain a capital letter on a typewriter. This will take time and practice.

If there are several ways to move the cursor, teach one only to start with, and add others later to reduce confusion.

If your student does not know the keyboard, you may worry that they will never learn. In fact, it is highly probable that your computer function may only use relatively few of the keys available, so concentrate on these and do not worry about the rest. They will come in time, and often sooner than you expect.

If your student is an ex-secretary, for example, and is a touch typist, the main problem will be slowing down their hands. Their fingers will move so quickly that you will have difficulty seeing what they are doing, and it will be difficult to see where they have made mistakes by pressing a wrong key.

Ex-secretaries also need to learn that they really must use the numeral 1, and not a lower case L. The same goes for zero: it really must be a nought, not a capital O. Very few secretaries use the numerals as they should, because for so long there was neither 1 nor 0 on the keyboard. Even now, one is never quite sure whether the golfball in use actually has '1' on it or '=' instead. Likewise, '0' could easily produce '¼'. Apart from this, you should have no major problems with touch typists, other than a desire to centre material on the screen in the way they are accustomed to on a typewriter. On a computer it may not matter, and may also be more trouble than it is worth.

The 'crib sheets' you use (see Figure 8.2) should include Key Learning Points, which will vary according to what you are teaching. Things like 'The cursor corrects to its left' are fairly standard, and very important. On a spreadsheet program, such as Visicalc or Supercalc, the importance of formulae is a definite Key Learning Point. Anything to do with health and safety is a Key Learning Point and should be emphasised and repeated.

Try to create an atmosphere which will encourage people to ask questions, and ask questions yourself to check understanding, such as 'Why do you use inverse video for these headings?' Finally, at the end of a training session try to finish on an upbeat, by giving people something to take away with them if possible. This is particularly important in the early stages, when people tend to lack confidence. A printout of the work they have done is a tremendous motivator.

People will almost always say they have forgotten all they learned between sessions. All you need to do is say 'Well, do something you can remember from last time – anything at all.' Generally, they will gingerly touch a key or two, which will lead to another and another and they will soon find that they have remembered almost everything. If there are gaps, however, enter them in the 'Special difficulties' section on the training record form. Finally, do not be afraid of spending as much as 25 per cent of the lesson time reminding your student of what they learned last time.

Keeping the interest up

There is a well-known plateau which all trainees reach at one time or another. This is the point at which, after some rapid learning, they consolidate what they have covered rather than extending their skills. At this stage the danger is that boredom will set in and you may need to use all your ingenuity to prevent this, or to overcome it. Keep telling your trainee the good news: they are doing fine, keep up like this and they will soon be doing more advanced work. Some organisations give a pay rise on reaching a certain proficiency level. If you just let them stay on the plateau, saying nothing specific and adding no variety, they will quickly lose interest. Keep standards up, because it is at the learning plateau that careless and slipshod habits tend to set in, the sort of habits which Nellie picks up and passes on, and this is one of the main reasons why you are doing this training yourself, and not relying on the time-honoured 'sit by Nellie' method.

Evaluating your training

There are four ways you can establish the success or otherwise of your training:

- It should increase productivity in the department. Work should go through faster, with fewer hold-ups and greater accuracy.
- Your trainee should find the job easier to do because you have provided training in the correct way to use equipment designed to remove much of the drudgery and monotony from the job as it was.
- Resulting from the above, your staff should

enjoy their work more. They should feel that they are in possession of more advanced skills and more sophisticated techniques. This should, and usually does, increase motivation and commitment with greater enthusiasm for the job, with correspondingly better performance.

● Training should be a means by which you develop your staff so that they are more easily promotable. You may regret the promotion of your most able staff, but you gain the reputation of being a 'good gardener', someone who grows good people and gives them opportunities to stretch and develop their skills and personalities. This has the effect of making you a magnet for other good staff who will want to work with you because of the chances for development which people receive when they work in your section or department.

The final question in evaluating the training you have given your staff is 'Would I pay for the quality of training I am giving my staff?' If you feel that your own training skills are on a par with training services available on the open market, you can feel satisfied that you are doing a good job.

USING OUTSIDE TRAINING SERVICES

It is useful to keep a file on training services available outside your own organisation as a back-up in an emergency. However, since the quality of these institutions varies a great deal, here are a few questions you should ask to make sure you are choosing the best:

1   What qualifications do your tutors have?
2   How long is it since your tutors spent time
    working in industry or commerce?
3   Do your tutors do other jobs (ie moonlighting)
    which brings them to your students tired and
    stale?
4   Do you train for other employers on a contract
    basis, and may I speak to them about the
    services offered?
5   Does each student have a machine of his or her
    own or will they have to share?
6   What documentation is provided? Is a copy
    available for each student? Is it a poor-quality
    photocopy, barely legible?
7   When reference is made to 'hands-on' training,
    whose hands do you refer to: the teacher's or
    the student's?

TRAINING YOUR STAFF: A SUMMARY

Training is an ongoing process at all levels. At top
management level group sessions are helpful, while
the desk-top training of subordinates should be
carried out in a relaxed, efficient atmosphere which
gives confidence to the trainee. Training records are
an important part of the job, and supervisors should
never neglect their own training and updating in the
technologies in use and planned for the future.
Finally, select outside training sources with care.

Further reading

Computers and Commonsense
R Hunt & J Shelley
Prentice-Hall International Inc., London
ISBN 0-13-165-399-7

Mastering Computers
G G L Wright
Macmillan Master Series (Paperback)
ISBN 0-333-30908

The Electronic Office
Dennis Jarrett
Gower Publishing Co Ltd/Philips Business
Systems
ISBN 0-566-03409-3

The Micro Revolution
Peter Laurie
Futura Publications Ltd
ISBN 0-7088-1794-7

Introducing Word Processing
G L Simons
NCC Publications
ISBN 0-85012-320-8

The Computer Book
Robin Bradbeer, Peter De Bono, Peter Laurie
BBC
ISBN 0-563-16484-0

Planning Office Automation — Electronic Message Systems
J A T Pritchard, P A Wilson
NCC
ISBN 0-85012-331-3

Tomorrow's Office Today
D W Birchall, V J Hammond
Business Books
ISBN 0-09 144920-0

This is IT
J Eaton, J Smithers
Philip Allan

Minis & Micros
The Institute of Production Engineering

Data Processing and Computer Studies
G Willmott
Edward Arnold
ISBN 0-7131-0746-4

Glossary

Access time
Quoted usually in terms of fractions of a second, it is the average speed with which data can either be read from or written to a disc surface. It varies with systems and manufacturers and is a function of hardware performance.

Acoustic coupler
A device into which a phone receiver is fitted so that digital pulses can be sent down phone lines and computers can 'talk' to each other.

Alphanumeric
Characters based on both letters and numerals (and often arithmetic signs, punctuation marks etc).

Application software
A program which carries out a specific required function (eg stock control, payroll, traffic control).

Archival storage
Filing of data stored for historical purposes which is high in volume but accessed infrequently.

Author
Usually a manager or executive who creates letters, reports etc. for word processing; someone who 'consumes' the product of word processors.

Automatic typewriter
Typewriter which can record on magnetic card for later playback with limited text editing facility.

Background
Some computers, and some word processors, can do only one thing at a time. Some have a background mode in which, for instance, printing and/or storing new documents can proceed while the keyboard is being used for the next entry job.

Backing storage
Storage of information and programs which are not required immediately for carrying out tasks on a computer-based system, but are accessed more frequently than archival material.

Bandwidth
The term for the telecommunications capability of a transmission link. If a bandwidth is 'wider' or 'higher' this increases the volume of information that it can carry; for example, with TV this could mean more channels.

BASIC
The most easily learnt of the high level languages and hence the most popular among microcomputer people. It is an acronym for Beginners' All Purpose Symbolic Instruction Code.

Batching
Collecting work of a similar nature to be processed at one time.

Bit
All computers work by the rapid manipulation of binary digits of which bit is an abbreviation.

Buffer
Temporary storage area where information can be assembled and/or held before the next operation.

Byte
A collection of eight bits which is interpreted by the computer as a decimal number or an alphanumeric character. 1k byte is a thousand (1,024 to be precise) of these.

CAD
Short for Computer Aided Design. An expensive technique usually requiring masses of computer power to build up complex graphics which are sometimes three dimensional representations.

Centre
(1) The word sometimes used to describe a department which was once a typing pool but is now a word processing centre.
(2) A command given to a word processor to centre automatically some part of the material on a page.

COBOL
An acronym for Common Business Oriented Language. More standardised than BASIC, it is the most popular commercial language on machines bigger than micros.

Command
Instructions given to word processors or computers to carry out certain functions.

Command key
A key on the keyboard specifically dedicated to use for a particular command.

Compiler
A program which translates the high level languages programmers use into the binary which computers use. It translates the entire program in one go.

Continuous stationery
Concertina-folded stationery for feeding on to a printer automatically. It may carry peel-off letter-headed paper, or carbonised paper. Needs a tractor-feed with sprocket holes to ensure accurate alignment.

CPU
Central processing unit: that part of a computer which does the work of translating human-readable data, manipulating it according to a program, storing and retrieving it, and turning it back into intelligible text as required.

Crash
A disc crash is an unfortunate occurrence, common to both floppy and hard discs (qv). It is caused by an obstruction between the disc surface and the read/write head. Although hard disc heads ride on a microscopic air cushion, floppy disc heads rest on the disc surface. Either way, any small particle, be it a condensation droplet, particle of smoke, or a speck of dust, can interrupt passage of the heads over the disc.

CRT

Cathode Ray Tube. The part of the terminal which actually displays data. More commonly used in the USA, in the UK the term VDU or VDT is more usual.

Cursor

The blip on the VDU screen showing where the next number or letter will appear.

Daisy wheel

Print element used on printers. A character is fixed on to the end of each 'petal', which impacts on to the paper as it passes through the roller. Daisy wheels may be metal or plastic and are available in a variety of typefaces and pitches, or characters per inch of type.

Database

A pool of cross-referenced information which the computer can draw on. It may be regarded as an electronic library.

Debug

To eliminate hardware of software errors from a system.

Digital

Information stored, transmitted and processed within electronic office systems, exists in a binary digital code.

Document

Name usually given to each item of text on a word processor.

Dot matrix
A low-quality printer which forms characters from a series of dots.

Editing
Altering in any way text stored on a word processor, eg deleting or inserting words, sentences or paragraphs, or moving any of these to another part of the document.

Electronic typewriter
Typewriter with limited storage and editing capabilities and automatic playback.

Facsimile
Usually abbreviated to FAX. Long distance photocopying down a telephone line, received in hard copy at the other end. May be sent overseas as well as locally.

Fanfold
Similar to continuous stationery (qv).

File
A set of data usually held on disc or tape backing store. It will normally have a structure being made up of many records (qv).

Floppy disc
Another removable storage medium. The discs are floppy but are encased in a cardboard packet like a record sleeve. Material is recorded on a magnesium oxide surface. Small discs (5½ inch diameter) can store up to 90 kBytes and larger ones (8 inch diameter) can store about 300 kB, that is, about 120 pages of A4.

Global search and replace
Facility found on most word processors allowing the replacement or alteration of the same word throughout an entire document, by the use of one command.

Hard copy
Paper version of material stored on a computer or word processor.

Hard disc
Also known as the Winchester disc, it is a high capacity storage medium which can store up to 8 million characters per side on an 8-inch disc. It is fixed into the computer, preventing corruption by dust, grease etc. by using a hermetic seal.

Hardware
The various mechanical, electrical, electronic and magnetic parts of a computer or word processor.

High level language
Nobody, except a computer, can cope with many binary digits at a time. Instead, a computer looks after the business of translating your code into noughts and ones. High level languages are codes more or less like English which are used on many different computers. BASIC and COBOL are examples.

Inkjet
A form of printing where a minute spray of ink is directed on to paper in the printer. Program controls are used to vary the type face. Quieter than impact daisy-wheel printers, but can be temperamental in daily use.

Input
Material or data which is entered on to a computer or word processor.

Input device
Means by which input is entered: keyboard, wand, voice, Optical Character Reader (qv).

Justification
Lines of type spaced to provide a flush right-hand margin, level all the way down the page, as is usual with left-hand margins.

Keyword search
An indexing system using words representative of the content of the information required.

LAN
Abbreviation for Local Area Network, in which linked computers access and transmit data within the confines of an office building.

Language
Means by which a programmer communicates with a computer. A low-level language is close to what the computer can directly understand. A high-level language is user-oriented (sometimes resembling English).

Main frame
A large computer having a wide range of facilities. Usually the largest computer in any particular system.

Main memory
This is a high-speed electronic device which holds the programs and information needed to carry out a specific task.

Media
Material used to store information or text, eg discs, tapes or magnetic cards.

Menu
A list of options, one of which can be selected by the operator.

Mercury
A national fibre-optic network intended to link large computers together. It is being set up by Cable and Wireless independently of British Telecom.

Merge
Combine information from different files which are stored on two discs, or on a single disc. Sometimes, paragraphs are taken from a library of paragraphs to form an individualised document. Alternatively, addresses from one file can be merged with standard letters from another, to form individual letters, frequently used for mailshots.

Microcomputer
Small computer using microprocessor technology. May include word processing facilities.

Microprocessor
Circuits which actually effect arithmetical and logical functions within the computer or computer-based device. The circuits are etched on to silicon chips, which are about ½ inch square, and wafer-thin.

Minicomputer
Middle-range computer, between a microcomputer and a mainframe in size. Some microcomputers can now out-perform minicomputers.

Modem
Short for modulator/demodulator, which takes digital pulses from a computer device and converts them into analogue bleeps to go down a phone line. At the other end of the line the bleeps are demodulated back into digits.

Multitasking
A mode of computer system operation in which two or more processes (programs) may operate concurrently, sharing the use of a processor.

Multi terminal system
A computer system utilising a number of user consoles which may access and update the same files of information.

Operating system/operating software
Means by which the running of the hardware is controlled. Provides an environment in which translators and applications software can run. Examples are DOS, CP/M.

Optical Character Reader (OCR)
A device which scans, reads and converts printed material into a form in which it can be read on to a screen for editing and/or storage on a computer or word processor.

Pagination
Automatic numbering and ejection of pages during printing, available on some word processors.

Peripheral
The generic name for the equipment outside a computer where information is fed in and out. Printers, VDUs, keyboards, floppy discs, tape drives and cartridges are all different kinds of peripherals.

Port
A socket into which a printer or some other device can be plugged.

Printer
A device, usually separate from the computer, which prints out in hard copy (qv) material required by the author. Some printers print a whole line at a time, and are known as line printers.

Program
The instructions which tell a computer what to do. Written in high or low level languages.

PSS
Packet switched service, British Telecom's public data network.

Qwerty keyboard
The standard typewriter keyboard which has been in use since 1876.

RAM
Random Access Memory. It is the place where information is temporarily stored while it is waiting to be manipulated by the CPU (qv).

Record
An item of data which has a fixed format. It will be made up of several fields, eg a record for personal details might have fields for name, address, age, sex, grade, salary.

Response time
An alternative term for access time (qv).

ROM
Read Only Memory, usually of semiconductor fabrication, the contents of which cannot be modified by the computer in which it is used.

Sectors
Used in connection with floppy discs and refers to the way that the disc is organised into 'wedges' or radial divisions which, along with the track number, provide the address of a piece of stored information.

Shared logic
Configuration of hardware in which several screens share a single CPU and printer (qv).

Sheet feed
A device attached to a printer, by which paper can be fed sheet by sheet on to the printer. Dual sheet feeders are also available. Sometimes called a hopper feed.

Silicon chip
Printed circuit, reduced and printed on a silicon wafer. When many circuits are built up in this way, a microprocessor is formed.

Software
Term used to describe programs or instructions telling a computer what to do.

Standalone
A word processor with its own keyboard, screen, CPU and printer independent of any other equipment.

Store and forward
A type of electronic mail system where messages can be sent from a work station and stored on the computer until the recipient at another work station asks for it to be forwarded when he or she is ready to deal with the message.

Switched
In telecommunications terms, it means that information, be it telephone or data, is passed through a central clearing point for subsequent access at widely distributed locations.

Syntax
The rules of a language which determine whether or not a statement is a valid use of the language. Syntax does not tell you whether the use to which you are putting the language is sensible, it only prevents you from creating invalid commands.

System software
Software provided to make the computer easier for the programmer to use.

Teletex
An advanced form of telex, faster and with facility for linking to word processors.

Teletext
Text displayed on TV screens and disseminated, like TV programmes, through the ether.

Terminal
A device allowing communication between a computer and an operator some distance away. Similar to a peripheral.

Text
Product or output of a word processor.

Turnkey system
Hardware and software which can immediately be set into useful action.

Underscoring
Automatic underlining of characters on computers or word processors.

Utility program
A program which has some function of general use to a programmer or user of the computer. Good examples would be programs to copy files or initialise discs.

VDU
Visual Display Unit, usually housed in a terminal (qv) allowing communication between terminals, and displaying material being input. (See also CRT.)

Volatile memory
Read/write memory whose content is lost when electrical power is turned off.

Word processor
A specialised type of computer which processes text
rather than information and numbers. Some word
processors handle limited amounts of numerical
data, with some information handling capacity.

Index